The
Reference Shelf®

Internet Safety

Edited by Richard Joseph Stein

The Reference Shelf
Volume 81 • Number 2
The H.W. Wilson Company
New York • Dublin
2009

The Reference Shelf

The books in this series contain reprints of articles, excerpts from books, addresses on current issues, and studies of social trends in the United States and other countries. There are six separately bound numbers in each volume, all of which are usually published in the same calendar year. Numbers one through five are each devoted to a single subject, providing background information and discussion from various points of view and concluding with a subject index and comprehensive bibliography that lists books, pamphlets, and abstracts of additional articles on the subject. The final number of each volume is a collection of recent speeches, and it contains a cumulative speaker index. Books in the series may be purchased individually or on subscription.

Library of Congress has cataloged this serial title as follows:

Internet safety / edited by Richard Joseph Stein.
 p. cm.—(The reference shelf ; v. 81 no. 2)
 ISBN 978-0-8242-1089-2 (alk. paper)
 1. Internet—Security measures. 2. Internet—Safety measures. 3. Computer crimes. 4. Internet—Political aspects. 5. Computers and family. I. Stein, Richard Joseph.
 TK5105.875.I57I5735 2009
 364.16'8—dc22

                                                                                    2009007443

Cover: Log on to the Internet. Photo by Daisuke Morita/Getty Images

Visit H.W. Wilson's Web site: www.hwwilson.com

Printed in the United States of America

Contents

Preface

Over the last dozen years, the growth of the Internet has been rapid and extensive. From shopping to socializing, blogging to photo-sharing, its uses have become tremendously varied, and it's now a major part of everyday life. As of 2006, nearly 75 percent of U.S. households had Internet access. The Internet has become nearly as culturally ubiquitous as television. In fact, many young people are foregoing television altogether, instead watching their favorite programs and movies on-line. As people rely more and more on computers for conducting day-to-day affairs, security becomes increasingly important. Networks are not always impregnable and are prone to infiltration by hackers, terrorists, and other predators. As Internet growth continues, protecting networks will remain a serious undertaking.

Divided into five chapters, this volume of the Reference Shelf series covers issues relating to Internet safety, including viruses, spam e-mails, Internet hoaxes, cyberbullying, identity theft, and international cyberterrorism. A particular emphasis is placed on answering the question: How do you protect yourself from what can seem like an endless array of on-line threats? As Internet growth has exploded, so too has cybercrime, the perpetrators of which have become ever more savvy, consistently staying one step ahead of those security measures designed to thwart their efforts. Armed with little more than laptop computers, clever criminals have the power to steal sensitive information, such as Social Security and bank-account numbers, as well as hack into and alter Web sites. Meanwhile, sexual predators have taken to such social-networking sites as Facebook and MySpace, looking for potential victims. While the Internet is not without its safeguards—firewalls, antivirus software, filters, administrators, etc.—none are foolproof.

The first chapter, "Safety in Numbers? An Overview of Internet Safety," provides a general synopsis of Internet safety, introducing many of the dangers that can be found on the Web. Selections in the second chapter discuss computer viruses, spam, and netbots, all three of which can infect computers. On a global scale, nearly 14.5 million spam e-mail messages are sent each day. Many of these contain viruses, which, given their ability to shut down entire networks, are cause for concern. Several of the articles highlight safety measures capable of protecting computers from such attacks.

Each year, some nine million people become the victims of identity theft, a form of crime that is the focus of chapter three. On-line identity theft involves criminals stealing personal information over the Web and using it for financial gain. The selected articles examine how high-tech thieves operate and offer helpful hints for keeping information private.

Internet safety for young people is a sensitive topic that generates extensive media coverage. Articles in the fourth chapter, "Internet Safety for Teens and Children," explore the many on-line dangers specific to young people. Among the topics discussed is peer-to-peer "cyberbullying," a phenomenon that has transferred the social antagonisms of the schoolyard to the comparatively unsupervised environs of cyberspace. This new form of harassment can have dire consequences, as is evidenced by the story of Megan Meier, a 13-year-old girl who, after being bullied on-line, took her own life. Selections in this chapter also focus on sexual predators, older individuals who uses the Internet as a tool to exploit children and teens.

Selections in the fifth and final chapter, "New Ways of War: Cyberattacks," discuss the threat of cyberwarfare worldwide. Increasingly dangerous and sophisticated, cyberattacks and cyberespionage prey on humanity's dependence on electronic communication and computer technology, finding and exploiting the flaws in these structures. These attacks often target defense systems and financial institutions and are employed by terrorists and governments alike. As an implement of war, the cyberattack lacks the obvious destructive power of a bomb or missile, but the chaos it creates can be every bit as deadly, crippling economies and shutting down governments. Cyberattacks are also used to steal classified or sensitive information, making it possible for military secrets to be intercepted, sold to the enemy, or even erased. Essential infrastructures, such as those linked to the distribution of energy, food, and water, are also vulnerable.

While the Web has transformed our world for the better and will continue to play a vital role in our shared future, Internet safety is a serious matter. Those with an on-line presence need to be aware of the potential dangers in order to protect themselves and fully enjoy all the benefits of the Internet Age.

Included in this volume is a bibliography detailing the books, Web sites, and periodical articles where additional information on Internet safety can be found.

In conclusion, I would like to extend a "thank you" to my colleagues at the H. W. Wilson Company, especially Paul McCaffrey, Kenneth Partridge, and Carolyn Ellis. Kudos also go to the authors and publishers who granted permission to reprint their articles in the book.

Richard Joseph Stein
April 2009

1

Safety in Numbers?
An Overview of Internet Safety

Editor's Introduction

Internet safety is an issue that affects individuals, schools, governments, and infrastructures. The articles in this chapter provide an overview of this important subject, introducing many of the topics that will be explored in later chapters.

In the first article, "Importance of Cybersecurity Increases as Online Attacks Get More Dangerous," Daniel Fowler examines the federal response to cyberthreats. In particular, he discusses the Comprehensive National Cybersecurity Initiative, a federal program authorized by President Bush in 2008 to safeguard government computer networks. On-line attacks have become more sophisticated and widespread, and a special federal commission has advocated creating a cybersecurity department akin to the Department of Homeland Security.

In "Newly Nasty," a writer for *The Economist* reports that computer networks are extremely vulnerable to on-line attacks. Government networks are better protected than those found on the World Wide Web, but even so, they are not immune. The article focuses on a 2007 assault on Estonia's Internet network. The incident crippled the country's digital infrastructure and spurred multinational discussions of a proposed global cybersecurity treaty.

Malware is software that damages an individual's computer. It is a form of hacking, much like a computer virus. In the third article, "Browsers: The New Threat Landscape," Andrew Garcia considers the different forms of malware and what IT departments can do to protect against them.

Marji McClure discusses security on the next generation of the Internet, or Web 2.0, in her article "Web 2.0 Security." She identifies Web 2.0's vulnerabilities and considers how the social-networking and communication capacities of the Web bring people together, fostering an openness that, while largely beneficial, economically and socially, nevertheless carries certain risks.

In her article "Deleting Your Digital Past," Tracy Mayor explains why it's crucial to maintain a good on-line reputation. Now that businesses regularly search the Web for information on both potential and current employees, Mayor writes, it has become important to keep one's on-line profile free from notoriety. Enter on-line reputation-management firms, which aim to help clients delete embarrassing photos, pieces of writing, and other cyber footprints.

The tragic case of 13-year-old Megan Meier is one of the most notorious instances of Internet excess in recent memory. Lori Drew, the mother of a friend of Meier's, posed as a 16-year-old boy on MySpace and struck up an on-line correspondence with Megan in order to find out whether she was saying anything negative about her child. Eventually, Drew's male alter-ego turned on Megan. Soon after, Megan committed suicide. In "Dead Teen's Mother: Misdemeanor

Convictions a 'Stepping Stone' in Cyberbullying Case," Kim Zetter explores the case and its implications.

The final two pieces in this chapter are excerpted from *The National Strategy to Secure Cyberspace*, a document formulated by the U.S. Department of Homeland Security in 2003 to address the new threats that have sprung up as a result of the development and evolution of the Internet. The first selection, "Cyberspace Threats and Vulnerabilities," charts these emerging threats, while the second entry, "National Policy and Guiding Principles," outlines the government's proposed response to them.

Importance of Cybersecurity Increases as Online Attacks Get More Dangerous[*]

By Daniel Fowler
Congressional Quarterly, October 19, 2008

When the federal government publicized its new cybersecurity strategy earlier this year, it was a signal moment—a firm acknowledgment that national security had intruded on the once-carefree realm of the Internet.

Established in January by presidential directive, the Comprehensive National Cybersecurity Initiative is a 12-point, multi-agency plan to secure the government's networks. The program aims, among other things, to reduce the number of federal network connections from more than 4,000 to about 100.

In September, Energy Department officials said that sensitive but unclassified information at some of the nation's science laboratories is vulnerable to attack and that cybersecurity experts were actually able to penetrate their networks during drills. The danger at the labs is seen as just one small example of a threat that cuts across the entire federal government.

"It's clear that we've been struggling or debating this issue for sometime now, and for the first time in the nation's history, I think we've got not only a coordinated interagency strategy, but we've got implementation plans, we've got budgets," said Robert Jamison, undersecretary of the Homeland Security Department's National Protection and Programs Directorate.

The strategy, portions of which remain classified, serves to address an ever-evolving problem. Where once spam and denial of service were the major concerns of businesses and government, attacks have become more sophisticated and more dangerous, experts say.

"The times have really changed," said Greg Garcia, the department's assistant secretary for cybersecurity and communications. "We're seeing now phishing, farming, botnets . . . war dialing and domain server spoofing. And we're seeing coordinated cyber-attacks against nation states."

Some of the more sophisticated methods involve techniques such as hijacking a computer and making it part of a "zombie" network, and mining passwords and sensitive personal information by posing as a trusted source in an e-mail.

In the past two years, there have been attacks against Estonia and Georgia emanating from Russia and hackers from China accessing U.S. federal government systems.

According to an Office of Management and Budget (OMB) report issued in March, federal agencies reported 12,986 cyber-incidents—everything from unauthorized access to malicious code—to DHS in fiscal 2007, up 152 percent from the previous year. The greatest increase was in events considered "unconfirmed and warranting further review" and can be attributed to "intensive analysis of suspicious traffic" picked up by the so-called Einstein network monitoring system sensors, according to the report.

"The whole area of cybersecurity is a challenge just because of the complexity of the issue and how networked we are, not only as a government, but also as a nation, so I mean the issue is a huge challenge," Jamison said.

Figuring out how best to work with the private sector, where 85 percent of the nation's critical infrastructure is located, and determining who should be in charge are among the immediate challenges.

Members of the Commission on Cybersecurity for the 44th Presidency, a project of the Center for Strategic and International Studies, say cybersecurity has become such a critical issue that management needs to take place at the highest level—in the White House—rather than at Homeland Security, as is now the case.

"It's very easy for individuals in the intelligence community or the defense community or other civilian agencies to dismiss the advice of DHS," said commission member Paul Kurtz, a partner at Good Harbor Consulting and a former special assistant to the president and senior director for critical infrastructure protection in the Bush administration.

While the commission hasn't finalized its recommendations, Kurtz said it is considering a model that involves creating a cybersecurity office within the Executive Office of the President. In that scenario, the director and other staff members could be "dual-hatted" to the National Security Council, others could be attached to OMB, and some might work only in the new office, he said.

Jamison at Homeland said that the White House is already involved and that the existing structure is working.

"I think DHS, with the resources that we're building, is positioned to take on the challenge, and I think any discussion about reorganization of roles and responsibilities actually takes us a step back instead of a step forward," he said.

While the presidential candidates have been mum on virtually all details of homeland security policy, whoever is in charge will have to figure out a way to bring the private sector under the security umbrella, either through partnerships, incentives or coercion.

"We need to develop security standards for the private industry that are mandated by the federal government," says Jeffrey F. Addicott, director of the Center for Terrorism Law at St. Mary's University School of Law in San Antonio. He says the federal government's engagement strategy doesn't work.

Larry Clinton, president of the Internet Security Alliance, a business group that focuses on collective Web security, says a "traditional regulatory model" won't succeed, either.

That model involves "prescriptions" proposed broadly in legislation, which are then turned over to an agency to promulgate into regulations, he said. Clinton recommends instead a system of economic incentives. "The government's role is to stimulate and motivate the owners and operators to appreciate that constantly improving information security is in their own self-interest," he said.

Andy Purdy, former acting director of the National Cybersecurity Division and a partner with Allenbaugh Samini, supports incentives and believes government and the private sector need to develop a stronger partnership. That would require, he said, a full risk assessment, articulation of what's needed for preparedness, a coordinated approach to cybercrime and malicious activity here and abroad, and a national research and development agenda.

"I think a key challenge is increasing the quality of the existing public-private partnership to get the private sector more completely engaged with the government," Purdy said.

Newly Nasty[*]

The Economist, May 26, 2007

Imagine that agents of a hostile power, working in conjunction with organised crime, could cause huge traffic jams in your country's biggest cities—big enough to paralyse business, the media, government and public services, and to cut you off from the world. That would be seen as a grave risk to national security, surely?

Yes—unless the attacks came over the internet. For most governments, defending their national security against cyberwarfare means keeping hackers out of important government computers. Much less thought has been given to the risks posed by large-scale disruption of the public internet. Modern life depends on it, yet it is open to all comers. That is why the world's richest countries and their military planners are now studying intensively the attacks on Estonia that started four weeks ago, amid that country's row with Russia about moving a Soviet-era war memorial.

Even at their crudest, the assaults broke new ground. For the first time, a state faced a frontal, anonymous attack that swamped the websites of banks, ministries, newspapers and broadcasters; that hobbled Estonia's efforts to make its case abroad. Previous bouts of cyberwarfare have been far more limited by comparison: probing another country's internet defences, rather as a reconnaissance plane tests air defences.

At full tilt, the onslaught on Estonia was also of a sophistication not seen before, with tactics shifting as weaknesses emerged. "Particular 'ports' of particular mission-critical computers in, for example, the telephone exchanges were targeted. Packet 'bombs' of hundreds of megabytes in size would be sent first to one address, then another," says Linnar Viik, Estonia's top internet guru. Such efforts exceed the skills of individual activists or even organised crime; they require the co-operation of a state and a large telecoms firm, he says. The effects could have been life-threatening. The emergency number used to call ambulances and the fire service was out of action for more than an hour.

For many countries, the events of the past weeks have been a loud wake-up call. Estonia, one of the most wired nations in Europe, actually survived pretty well. Other countries would have fared worse, NATO specialists reckon.

National security experts used to dealing with high-explosives and body counts find cyberwarfare a baffling new theatre of operations. In Estonia's case, "botnets" (swarms of computers hijacked by surreptitiously placed code, usually spread by spam) swamped sites by deluging them with bogus requests for information. Called a "distributed denial of service" (DDOS) attack, this at its peak involved more than 1m computers, creating traffic equivalent to 5,000 clicks per second on some targets. Some parts were highly co-ordinated—stopping precisely at midnight, for example. Frank Cilluffo, an expert formerly at the White House, says that the attack's signature suggests that more than one group was at work, with small-time hackers following the initial huge sorties.

Most countries have been complacent about guarding information infrastructure. In America, a congressional committee for computer security has given failing grades to many of the federal bodies it scrutinises. The Department of Homeland Security supposedly has a "cybersecurity czar" but the throne has not yet found a steady occupant.

Private firms have had more experience in fighting off internet attacks. Organised crime gangs, often from Eastern Europe, extort money from gambling and pornography sites by using botnets to make them unreachable. Last week a large DDOS attack hit YLE, Finland's public broadcaster. This week Britain's *Daily Telegraph* was hit. No political or financial motive was apparent. A Romania-based hacker led the Finnish attack.

Firms of varying competence and credibility peddle technical solutions. The typical protection against DDOS attacks is to buy lots of extra computers and bandwidth to handle an unexpected spike in traffic. "Mirroring" content across several servers means the cyber-attackers must hit many more targets simultaneously before disrupting anything. A system's architecture helps too: Estonia's open approach, with its built-in flexibility and resilience, and co-operation between the state, business and academics, worked well. Mr Viik hopes this will deter those trying to build cyberdefences on a military or state monopoly model.

Counterattacks are possible, but tricky. Security firms' staff can pose as hackers to infiltrate cybergangsterdom. This used to be a mere battle of wits. Now there are real fears of violence. "It's changed now that big money is involved. It is not beyond the realm of imagination that someone might be targeted," says Mikko Hyppönen of F-Secure, an internet security firm.

But technology and sleuthing offer only a partial fix. The real question facing industrialised countries is how to create a legal environment that counts cyberaggression not as a kind of practical joke, but a grave breach of the legal order, akin to terrorism, international organised crime, or aggression against another state.

NATO is rethinking its position. It is designed to protect members against physical attack. When Estonia appealed for help it could only send an observer to Tallinn to monitor the attacks. For now, informal alliances are more useful.

Internet companies in friendly countries such as Sweden headed off many of the attacks before they even reached Estonia. Ken Silva, the security chief at VeriSign, which runs big chunks of the internet's domain-name system, advocates defences at the core of the network to tackle malicious data-packets before they reach their target. But finding agreement among the world's privately run internet networks is hard.

The urgent need is for an international legal code that defines cybercrimes more precisely, and offers the basis for some remedies. The Council of Europe, a continent-wide talking-shop that is the guardian of many international legal conventions, has a treaty on cybercrime dating from 2001. Acceptance has been partial. From overseas, America and Japan have signed up; Russia so far hasn't.

The International Telecommunication Union, which unites all 191 countries that use the world telephone system, hopes to take the lead in pushing for a global convention against cybercrime. Alexander Mtoko, its expert on cyberwarfare, says the key issue is anonymity: "We are in an industry where there is no control, no rules, no identities—it's the wild west. But for critical applications you have to know who you are dealing with." NATO experts agree. At a minimum, any international cybercrime convention is likely to oblige internet service providers to co-operate in blocking DDOS attacks coming from their subscribers' computers.

Yet the underlying problem is the internet itself. Wreaking havoc with anonymous telephone calls is hard. The internet's inherent openness allows hackers to hide. Yet that also helps make it cheap and innovative. Some countries may be more willing than others to trade freedom for security.

Mr Viik thinks a new global cybersecurity treaty may be reached by 2012. But victory will never be complete, thanks to the asymmetry between cat and mouse, notes Bruce Schneier, a security expert. "It is easier to come up with a new attack than with a new defence," he says. The strongest defence, says Mr Cilluffo, may be resilience: "the ability to reconstitute quickly, recover and absorb."

Browsers[*]

The New Threat Landscape

By Andrew Garcia
eWeek, August 4, 2008

With web-borne threats and drive-by downloads becoming the most trouble-some form of malware today, enterprise IT administrators and users alike need to reconsider the tools and practices they prescribe and employ to protect computers and data—particularly as otherwise legitimate Web sites become the primary vector for malware transmission.

We've seen a twofold approach to malware as evildoers attempt to monetize their evildoings.

The first form stems from the phishing business, where malware authors create new domains and Web sites so fast that URL filtering and signature databases cannot keep up. The goal here is to score a few victims before the security companies can generate new signatures.

The second form consists of hijacked Web sites—sites that are otherwise legitimate but have been corrupted in a way that leads their visitors to malicious content.

An example of the interplay between these two types of Web threats is the Asprox botnet. The botnet originally derived from phishing attempts to draw unwitting users to malware via short-lived Web sites, but, in the last few months, Asprox has morphed into SQL injection attacks against legitimate sites. In automated fashion, the botnet leverages Google to find and exploit Web sites with vulnerable Active Server Pages, injecting an IFrame into the assailable site that redirects site visitors to exploit code elsewhere on the Web.

According to some sources, legitimate Web sites now comprise the majority of pages currently hosting malware. In its July 2008 Security Threat Report Update, Sophos Labs declared that 90 percent of the infected Web pages it detected in the first half of 2008 originated from legitimate Web sites that were hacked in some form. The report also stated that Sophos Labs found, on average, more than 16,000 new infected pages each day during that time.

The changes in the way malware is propagated necessitate changes in the way IT managers secure corporate assets and give advice to users on keeping safe.

If the legitimate Web sites a user visits regularly, such as banks, merchants or social networks, can no longer be trusted to be clean, the old "spam-oriented" rule—not clicking on links in e-mail—becomes less relevant.

Indeed, when legitimate Web sites are the major source of malware, and users cannot readily tell whether a site is trustworthy by looking at it, there needs to be a technological solution to fill the breach and provide some assurance to users that the sites they visit are safe at this very moment—not five months ago, not an hour ago, but now.

Security providers have been trying out many new technologies to combat the problem of Web threats, as older, signature-based detections of the file system performed by anti-virus platforms have proven ineffective against new types of threats.

Newer technologies layer on Web reputation validation, in-line Web traffic scanning and script-blocking technologies to a browser's extended capability set, while anti-virus vendors augment their own platforms with more heuristic and behavioral analysis features.

Most of these browser add-on technologies have been targeted squarely on the Wild West that is the consumer's Microsoft Windows-based PC. Corporate customers, to date, have not suffered as much from Web threats, as enterprise administrators have deployed a tiered phalanx of both network- and host-based security solutions to combat all types of threats.

For example, intrusion prevention appliances or an in-line Web gateway appliance can detect and block both outbound traffic that looks like botnet activity and inbound, malware-laden Web traffic. However, network-based solutions will not protect users as they go mobile, outside the corporate network perimeter.

Makers of security solutions geared toward enterprise customers have made strides to improve their built-in detection and analysis of Web network traffic—blocking code from touching a protected system by examining the way it behaves or identifying its similarities to known threats before it touches the file system.

There are different approaches that administrators will need to evaluate before making any kind of deployment decision. Some products plug into the browser to specifically examine how things such as ActiveX or JavaScript behave, while others perform a more holistic HTTP scan that determines whether a Web request was made from a browser, e-mail application or other source. Other solutions, meanwhile, are baked into enterprise security platforms.

Some security companies are also changing the model by which malware is identified. Trend Micro, for example, is moving from a signature push model—where signatures need to be updated frequently all over the network—to a request-time pull for threat information from the cloud.

FIX MIX

Enterprise IT may be tempted to delve into consumer-oriented tools to augment the security of their most exposed, remote workers. However, such experiments will be fraught with complications. With most of these products, there is no central management component, so each instance is managed and updated on a one-off basis. Also, the products vary in their support for different browsers, which could interfere with the operation of outdated but mission-critical Web applications.

The best practical, vendor-neutral advice I can offer to avoid Web threats is to keep your systems patched—and by this I mean the operating system, the browser and its add-ons, as well as applications. That said, browser updates can sometimes cause incompatibilities with legacy Web applications.

Security software itself can even punish companies that don't keep fully up-to-date. For example, one of my favorite Web site validation and scanning tools—the stand-alone version of AVG's LinkScanner Pro—does not yet support Firefox 3.0, more than a month after the release of Mozilla's latest browser.

In cases such as these, administrators must weigh the use of a security program versus the productivity gained by using the application itself (and productivity usually wins). But if a security company has been known to be slow to adapt to browser improvements, the security solution will likely be a bad fit for corporate use on an ongoing basis.

WEB 2.0 Security[*]

Getting Collaborative Peace of Mind

By Marji McClure
Econtent, November 2008

Web 2.0 applications have opened up a lot of communication channels—and opportunity—for business professionals. They can, more than ever before, reach out to individuals from across the globe and share content and web applications. Through blogs, wikis, and social networking sites such as Facebook and Linked In, people are becoming more and more electronically intertwined. "There's a sense of security in a Web 2.0 world where people trust their personal information to others," says Jordan Frank, VP of sales and marketing for Traction Software. "They trust these sites."

Frank points out that some people trust such systems just because their friends do, and because sites such as Facebook haven't let people down—yet. He cautions that a breach could cause a backlash against such networks. "Ensuring success in Web 2.0 means that trust doesn't get broken," says Frank.

Most companies don't want to inhibit the collaborative flow that Web 2.0 has brought with it; they don't want it to hinder their overall operations and they want to continue to build on their Web 2.0 platforms. A Gartner Executives Programs survey of 1,500 CIOs from across the globe revealed that half of the respondents expected to invest in Web 2.0 technologies for the first time in 2008.

Internet experts agree that part of that investment must include security measures to protect organizations' intellectual property. One reason that Web 2.0 garners more attention for security safeguards than its predecessors is that its open nature makes it naturally more vulnerable to breaches. "The fact that security is becoming an issue speaks to the growth that Web 2.0 applications are having in the business world," says Isaac Garcia, CEO and co-founder of Central Desktop, which offers a web-based business collaboration platform.

Companies need to recognize the fact that the benefits that new technologies afford are typically accompanied by challenges. Web 2.0 is no different in this regard than any other technology offering. "The key thing is that when you're rolling out new technologies, these new technologies bring new vulnerabilities, as well as renew old vulnerabilities," according to John Pescatore, VP of internet research at Gartner, Inc. "It's an important time to build security features."

THE IMPLICATIONS

Web 2.0 security goes beyond the content that users find on the web and share with others within their network. It also involves preventing data leakage; that is, ensuring that that content doesn't find its way out, notes William "Sandy" Bird, CTO for Q1 Labs. The main vulnerabilities can be found directly in the collaboration applications such as wikis and blogs, in syndication (from RSS feeds and mashups), as well as Rich Interface Applications (RIA) and AJAX-enabled websites. Web 2.0 applications are vulnerable to a variety of threats, from cookie tampering to cross-site scripting (XSS) attacks.

Oftentimes, when such attacks occur, the user is unaware that his computer—and important data—has been compromised. It's a different world from years ago when viruses would wreak immediate (and very obvious) havoc on computer users. The threat may be imperceptible, and potentially even more dangerous.

The potential for security breaches caused by Web 2.0 technology is not likely to go away on its own. As more and more individuals use these applications (especially in the workplace), the risk of suffering from security breaches will likely increase considerably. In fact, companies are facing security issues on both the client side and the server side, says Danny Allan, director of security research for IBM Rational. Both can have devastating effects on companies, their employees, and their customers when the data created and stored in these Web 2.0 environments is compromised.

"Web 1.0 was a static page. With Web 2.0, you've got more client-side processes, like AJAX and widgets. Technically, there's more going on," says Doug Camplejohn, CEO and founder of Mi5 Networks, which focuses on the client side of the security issue.

DON'T DROP YOUR GUARD

This collaborative environment seems to be one in which users have let their guards down. "People don't read licensing agreements, they'll add a widget or they'll click on a link," adds Camplejohn, noting that the "bad guys" have gotten better at making harmful applications look legitimate. What has also changed, notes Camplejohn, is that when a virus and spam infected a system, their effects were noticed immediately. "The new threats are silent," says Camplejohn. "They sneak in under the radar."

Mi5 Networks provides companies with Webgate appliances that help prevent vulnerabilities from occurring as well as helping to clean up any problems that do occur. The Webgate solutions don't require any installation and immediately monitor and block vulnerabilities. "Companies use us for two reasons: to see what employees are doing and what they are not doing; and to see what applications are okay and not okay," explains Camplejohn.

Imperva stresses the importance of having security measures in place on the server side when explaining its security solutions to customers. "What we talk to customers about is the need to apply security on the server side because that's where you have control," says Mark Kraynak, Imperva's director of strategic marketing. Still, with this approach, the goal is to prevent future problems. "We can show how the applications are working and we use the model to prevent attacks," explains Kraynak. Imperva's SecureSphere monitors the activity in its customers' applications and databases to prevent vulnerabilities. By using dynamic profiling, Imperva creates profiles of applications and databases, so changes and possible malicious activity can be more easily noticed.

Experts agree that such a proactive approach is the best approach, and one of the most popular solutions seems to be the technology that enables its clients to closely monitor its Web 2.0 systems and send alerts when a security breach is detected.

It's also helpful for companies to identify exactly who caused a security breach, and Q1 Labs' flagship product offers clients that visibility. QRadar enables its clients to uncover the source of a security problem and protect themselves against any security threats before they cause problems. "It's providing visibility to the incident as a whole," says Bird.

Most often, violators don't have malicious intentions, notes Camplejohn. However, safeguards still need to be in place to prevent users from accessing harmful websites and applications. Mi5 Networks has technologies that will block users from visiting a webpage that is identified as a risk. They receive a message that informs them that the particular page violates company policy. "We can also block a portion of a page and still deliver the good content," adds Camplejohn.

Pescatore notes that many organizations seek solutions that have security features already built in. He points to IBM and HP, which both purchased companies last year that offer security tools. IBM acquired Watchfire and HP bought SPI Dynamics. (Allan actually joined Watchfire in 2000 and transitioned to IBM with the acquisition.)

Within a few months, IBM released IBM Rational AppScan, which is a complete suite of automated web application security tools that scan and test web applications for security vulnerabilities. It also offers recommendations for how to fix problems that are identified, which helps organizations close the loop on their security issues.

SECURING ENTERPRISE 2.0

Frank notes that while security in the Web 2.0 world is focused more on the protection of personal information, Enterprise 2.0 security (or Web 2.0 in the Enterprise) is targeted on protecting information in the project or community work-space. "The matter of security goes beyond simple authentication—am I who I say I am?—and privacy control—who can see what information," says Frank. In addition to authentication, he notes that other important aspects of security include permissions/access control (What can you see and do in the environment?), an audit trail (What happened over time? When was a document emailed? What comments were included on it?), and monitoring (the ability for users to keep up-to-date on new activity). It also enables administrators to monitor harmful content and suppress it as it's posted.

Traction Software's flagship product is the Traction TeamPage hypertext platform that organizations use as the backbone of an online information-sharing system. Through it, Traction Software addresses all of these security issues.

More specifically, Traction Software's access control lists (ACLs) give server and project administrators the power to manage who accesses each project. The server ACL editor enables the assignment of server-level permissions to individual users and groups. There are permissions for such functions as emailing content out of the server or exporting content from the server to other formats (such as PDF). A project ACL editor controls functions such as what content an individual can author, contribute comments to, or read.

Central Desktop, a business collaboration platform where users can manage and collaborate their workspace in an online environment, launched a suite of security tools in early 2008 to help customers ensure the security of their data. The "security pack" add-on was designed to help these customers comply with both internal and external security issues. Central Desktop's security features include a strong password complexity layer (in which requirements such as using one lowercase letter are created). Passwords can also be programmed to automatically expire within a specified period of time (such as monthly). Security measures can also restrict access to a company's online environment to those with a specific IP address.

COMMITMENT REQUIRED

Just as collaboration in a Web 2.0 environment is a continuous process, security measures require the same diligence, experts agree. "This is not a one-time analysis," says Allan. "It needs to be continuous." Fortunately, the proactive approach that is necessary to have successful Web 2.0 security measures in place is catching on. "We're seeing the shift to the business owner starting to address the problem proactively," says Allan. "From experience, without fail, we find there is less vulnerability for those who take a proactive approach."

The solutions must still be easy for companies to integrate into their operations. "I can't say any customers are just buying it and forgetting about it," says Kraynak. "But it needs to be low maintenance." Kathleen Reidy, senior analyst for The 451 Group, notes how solutions such as the ones that Central Desktop offers provide companies with a slate of secure tools that have consumer-friendly functionality. So security becomes an easy process for them to control.

Companies are likely going to have to continue navigating themselves through the security issue, since they may not get a guiding hand from developers. "Developers are going to have to be more security-aware," says Kraynak. "But they are not motivated to do it; they're motivated by helping the business do better. They're not motivated to hold back the process for security."

"When you do this as part of the software development life cycle, it's being caught too late in the cycle," adds Allan. However, Pescatore says that more enterprises are testing software before it is even installed as a way to prevent potential security issues from occurring in the first place.

While Web 2.0 security features can create a more productive work environment, there are also financial benefits. What companies need to recognize, notes Allan, is that implementing security measures can serve as a competitive advantage. "It's a cost advantage—fixing things early in the cycle costs less," says Allan. "The majority of organizations need to build it into their processes."

Fortunately, this shift is occurring. Web 2.0 security solution providers say that they have seen an increased interest in security products from customers. They expect the need for such solutions will continue to grow as Web 2.0 applications are further developed and integrated into the workflow.

SECRECY—NOT SECURITY

Sites you visit during a private session generally won't be able to access cookies, history, or other browser data created or saved before you entered the session. IE 8s InPrivate has an additional blocking option that will prevent sites from sharing data about your visit with third-party data collectors, such as ad networks, that the browser Learns about during the course of your surfing, But no browser can prevent sites from tracking your visit. To hide yourself from sites, you need to use a service such as the for-pay Anonymizer or the free Tor. These new privacy features are all worthwhile, and they should all fit in with your everyday surfing much better than existing browser options (such as those that wipe out your entire browsing history). Just keep in mind that they're not a panacea, and that they're for secrecy, not additional safety.

Deleting Your Digital Past—For Good[*]

By Tracy Mayor
Computerworld, November 16, 2008

An unsavory connection from your past. An annoying link to your name that's dragging down your career. A spicy quote you tossed off to a reporter that you wish you could take back.

As time goes by, more of us are being tailed by some little thing out there on the Web, an awful bit that emerges when someone Googles our names, a black mark that we'd like to erase before a colleague or a prospective employer sees it.

A whole industry—known as online reputation management—has grown up around helping individual clients and corporate clients suppress negative information online by creating more positive and search-engine-friendly postings.

But what if you don't just want something massaged, manipulated or suppressed? What if you want it gone? Is it possible for an ordinary person to get some damaging tidbit entirely erased from the Web?

Computerworld decided to find out. We gave ourselves a week to try to expunge unwanted online mentions, using three real-life examples as test cases:

- **A recent college graduate with a distinctive last name would like to get rid of an entry on someone else's long-abandoned online journal**. The entry mentions her full name in a rambling tale of drug-induced debauchery and sexual high jinks. It always shows up as the fourth or fifth result in a Google search on her name—a real problem now that the young woman (let's call her WrongedGirl) is applying for jobs.

- **A freelance writer is mistakenly identified as a movie critic on Rotten Tomatoes, a popular site that aggregates movie reviews from print, TV and the Web**. Although she personally admires Rotten Tomatoes, she worries that her byline juxtaposed next to the word "rotten" in the first few Google search results sets up an unpleasant association in the minds of prospective clients—especially older business people who have no idea what Rotten Tomatoes is.

- **In an interview seven years ago, an IT professional gave a quote to *Computerworld* that included a salty phrase**. She recently contacted the editors, asking them to either remove her name from the piece or prevent the article from being found in a search. Her goal: "I don't want any hits at all when my name is searched."

We started by calling a couple of online image management professionals for some free advice.

WHAT NOT TO DO

If you're trying to get something erased from the Web, your first instinct might be to pursue legal action. Resist this urge, says Michael Fertik, CEO of ReputationDefender Inc., an online reputation management and privacy company in Redwood City, Calif.

Why? The Communications Decency Act of 1996 gives almost total immunity to Web sites, says Fertik. Even if you can establish a legal case, the distinctly nonphysical nature of the Web—where you, your defamer and the company that hosts the offending material can be in different states or countries, or simply be unknown—means that sorting out jurisdictions can turn into a legal quagmire.

Likewise, Fertik adds, another surprise dead end is the place where many people launch their erasure efforts: Google.

If an item doesn't show up in a Google search, it's as good as being truly gone, right?

Wrong. "Removing content from Google or another search engine would still leave the original content that exists on the Web," says a Google spokesman.

The better route, according to the spokesman: "Users that want content removed from the Internet should contact the webmaster of the page or the Internet hosting companies or ISPs hosting the content to find out their content removal policies."

STRIKE ONE: MISBEGOTTEN QUOTE

Computerworld started with three real-life instances in which people wanted material expunged from online sites, but the experts we consulted were optimistic about only one case—the situation in which a young woman's first and last name were included in a salacious online journal entry.

Here's a look at another case:

- **IT manager talks salty to a business publication—*Computerworld*—and later regrets it**. On this topic, our experts were divided. Columbia

University journalism professor Todd Gitlin says it would be exceedingly rare for any mainstream publication to change the record for any reason. (*Computerworld*'s editors agreed. The quote, with the source's name attached to it, still stands.)

ReputationDefender CEO Michael Fertik sees a little wiggle room, however. True, *The New York Times* is unlikely to change the record, but some smaller outlets might, he says.

"I don't know if I buy the journalistic integrity argument—though I respect it. A lot of small newspapers will fold right away as soon as you threaten them," he says.

That said, he notes that ReputationDefender does not handle requests to expunge material from mainstream media.

Google does offer tools on its support page to help with urgent requests to prevent personal content from appearing in a search result, such as when credit card or Social Security numbers are accidentally or maliciously published on the Web. If you do manage to successfully remove such an item, you'll need to also make sure that Google no longer caches the information, the representative says.

If legal action is prohibitively complicated and Google and other search engines can't help, what's the best tactic for getting something erased? A little digital digging and a lot of good old-fashioned human contact.

Priority No. 1 is to try to reach a human being, says Chris Martin, founder of ReputationHawk.com, an online reputation management service. His company starts by tracking down someone who has access to the Web site in question—either the author of the material or a third party like a webmaster or Web hosting service. "If the Web host is billing that person every month, if it's a paid account, they'll be able to contact them," Martin says.

THE TALKING CURE

If that approach fails, his company tries to reach people through various social media sites such as MySpace or Facebook or Web portals like Yahoo.

The bottom line: An address or a live e-mail account is good; a human on the phone is better, Martin says. "We call," he says. "We say we're from an Internet privacy corporation. We explain the situation, and we say, 'You need to take care of this as soon as possible.'"

Many times, people do, he says. "The situation can resolve really quickly," Martin says. "If there's a legitimate problem, it's natural for someone to go in there and take the material down."

ReputationHawk's fees vary by case. For a situation like WrongedGirl's, the charge would be $500 or less, Martin says. ReputationDefender doesn't take on ad hoc erasure cases. Instead, clients pay $9.95 per month for a yearly subscription and $29.95 per removal.

Both services claim that they have a much higher success rate than individuals. The reason? You're a newbie; they do this all day, every day.

ReputationDefender has taken on about 1,000 cases with an 85% success rate, according to Fertik. He says the cases build upon one another as relationships develop. "If you call them informally enough times, let them know you're not an abusive company, you're not sending legal letters, then you can have a very high success rate."

In contrast, says Martin, an individual trying to clean up his own reputation starts from scratch and has almost no clout. "We can dig and find contact information pretty quickly, and we're going to have a lot more pull when contacting the Web site owner," he says.

SETTING WRONGEDGIRL RIGHT

Of our three cases, both experts said the case of WrongedGirl stood the best chance of being resolved. That's good news, since it's the type of scenario that's playing out ever more frequently as the Net generation enters the workforce.

Armed with advice from the pros, we set out one recent Monday to see how far we could get in righting WrongedGirl's reputation in a week.

We first tried to track down the journal author herself, with the idea that we could entreat her to take down the offensive material. (Perhaps she had matured since her partying days.) It seems that five years ago, she set up an account at a free online journal site and posted half a dozen entries in 10 days—most apparently written under the influence of one substance or another—before abandoning the site.

We knew only her first name, her hometown from five years ago and the bands she liked at that time. The e-mail address listed in the user account for her online journal was defunct.

STRIKE TWO: ROTTEN TOMATOES

Our final attempt to erase someone's digital tracks also met with defeat.

- **Freelance journalist wants her name taken off the Rotten Tomatoes movie-review Web site.**

Good luck with that, say ReputationDefender Inc. CEO Michael Fertik, ReputationHawk founder Chris Martin and Columbia University journalism professor Todd Gitlin. Large, commercial (implication: lucrative) Web sites have little need to accommodate your petty requests. If you get through and find a sympathetic person on the end of a phone line, perhaps you'll get lucky. Otherwise, fuggedaboutit.

That prediction turned out to be on the money. Multiple e-mails to various Rotten Tomatoes addresses went unanswered or were bounced back as undeliverable. Messages left at the phone number for the parent company, IGN Entertainment Inc., likewise went nowhere.

Apparently, the journalist's best course of action would be to do what reputation mavens recommended in the first place: Create enough positive, search-engine-friendly content to push the "rotten + journalist's name" search result to Google's second page of results.

WrongedGirl provided us with a possible last name for the author, but unfortunately, like the author's first name, it was too common to be helpful. Her first and possibly last names together garnered 1,260 hits on Google, including multiple references on YouTube and multiple accounts on LinkedIn and Facebook, none of which appeared to be our author.

After a couple of mind-numbing hours trolling MySpace accounts, we did find an entry that looked promising (same first name, same state and county, if not exact hometown, and same favorite bands), but that too had been updated only a few times before being abandoned more than two years ago. It looked like we had a serial journaler on our hands.

We gave up on trying to track down the author and turned to the site where the journal was posted—Blurty. We posted our request to remove the offending material in the support forum. A few moments later, we received an automated e-mail response, with a tracking number, saying that our request had been received and would be addressed as soon as possible. But over the next four days, nobody responded.

SCOPING OUT THE SITE

Trying another angle, we trolled through Blurty's support, legal, privacy and terms of service documents and sent e-mails to any other addresses we found there (abuse@blurty.com, for example), asking that the entry in question be taken down.

Two days later, with no response on any front, we used WhoIs to try to find a physical address for Blurty. Its technical contact was listed as being in Encinitas, Calif. When we called the phone number given in the WhoIs listing, a recorded voice informed us we'd reached Sunlane Media LLC.

Back to the Web for more searching: Our heart sank when we found that Sunlane has registered hundreds of other domains, nearly all of which appeared to be porn sites. Wonderful.

We called three separate phone numbers we found for Sunlane in various WhoIs listings—two of which sounded like cell phones and one that had the quality of a home answering machine circa 1995. None had a live person on the other end. We left messages at each number, trying to sound professional enough to elicit a swift response and distressed enough to elicit sympathy.

RESOLUTION

The next day was Friday, our self-imposed deadline. We sent one final e-mail—replying to the webmaster address from which we'd received the tracking number earlier in the week—and requesting a response that leaned even more heavily on the sympathy angle.

Still nothing. At the end of the day, feeling discouraged, we drafted an e-mail to Fertik at ReputationDefender, requesting suggestions for further action. But when we Googled WrongedGirl's name to find and furnish the link to the offensive journal entry, it was gone from Google.

Amazed, we flipped over to the Internet Explorer bookmark we'd made for the page and saw this message: "Error. This journal has been suspended."

Excellent! But just what had done the job—which e-mail or phone call? We had no way of knowing, though a full 10 days later, an e-mail arrived from the abuse@ blurty.com address, telling us what we'd already figured out: The journal had been taken down.

HAVE YOUR SAY

We were ebullient but also chastened. Yes, we had managed restore WrongedGirl's good name, but we had no clear understanding of exactly how we had done it, and our other two attempts at erasing unwanted online tracks had come up dry.

In the end, Fertik's words came back to haunt us: "A lot of this stuff you can do yourself—if you have the time, the expertise and the temperament to get it done," he had told us before we began. "But how many people change the oil in their own car anymore?"

Of course, Fertik has a vested interest in urging people to hire companies like his own, but we had to concede that he also had a point: Erasing your tracks online takes time, perseverance and more than a little luck.

Dead Teen's Mother: Misdemeanor Convictions a 'Stepping Stone' in Cyberbullying Case[*]

By Kim Zetter
Wired, November 26, 2008

The mother of the 13-year-old girl who committed suicide following a MySpace hoax said she was satisfied with Wednesday's verdict in the resulting criminal prosecution, even though the jury rejected three felony computer hacking charges against the defendant, convicting her instead of minor misdemeanor counts. The jurors deadlocked on a fourth felony conspiracy charge.

Tina Meier, speaking at a press conference, said she had prepared herself for any verdict, but was "of course, wanting convictions on all of them." She called the misdemeanor convictions "a stepping stone" and said she wanted Drew to get prison time.

"Absolutely I think she needs to be punished," Meier said. "I would like the maximum three years."

On Wednesday, jurors found 49-year-old Lori Drew guilty of three misdemeanor counts of gaining unauthorized access to MySpace for the purpose of obtaining information on Megan Meier. Misdemeanors potentially carry up to a year in prison each, but more commonly result in little or no time in custody for a first offense. The jury unanimously rejected the three felony computer hacking charges that alleged the unauthorized access was part of a scheme to intentionally inflict emotional distress on Megan.

The federal prosecutor in charge of the cyberbullying case said he was also pleased with Wednesday's outcome.

The jury "held Lori Drew responsible," said U.S. Attorney Thomas O'Brien during a post-verdict press conference.

Drew's defense attorney, however, had harsh words for O'Brien.

"If he wants to take that as a victory, then God bless him," H. Dean Steward said.

Steward said his client should never have been charged with computer crimes, or anything else.

O'Brien "seems to think he's smarter than" prosecutors in Missouri "who chose not to bring charges against Drew," Steward said, adding that politics likely played a role in O'Brien's decision to prosecute the case himself. "O'Brien wants to continue to be U.S. attorney into the Obama administration, and he wants a victory for that reason," Steward said. "It's to his discredit" that he brought charges.

Drew was charged in Los Angeles County, where MySpace's computers are located, after officials in Missouri concluded Drew hadn't violated any existing state law.

Drew, of O'Fallon, Missouri, faced one count of conspiracy and three counts of unauthorized computer access for allegedly violating MySpace's terms of service by participating in the creation of a fake profile for a non-existent 16-year-old boy named "Josh Evans." Prosecutors said she conspired to create the account with her then-13-year-old daughter, Sarah, and a then-18-year-old employee and family friend named Ashley Grills. The account was used to emotionally manipulate 13-year-old Megan Meier, who later killed herself.

The four counts were charged as felonies, based on allegations that the "unauthorized access" was for the purpose of causing emotional harm to Megan. But jurors were also given the option of finding Drew guilty of misdemeanors if they found no such intent, determining instead that Drew was only trying to obtain information about the girl.

Each misdemeanor conviction can carry a fine of up to $100,000 in addition to the maximum possible prison sentence of up to a year.

The misdemeanor conviction implies that the jury believed Drew gained unauthorized computer access to MySpace's computer system, but did not do so to intentionally inflict emotional distress on Megan.

Both Ashley Grills and Sarah Drew had testified that the intent in creating the account was to lure Megan into conversation with "Josh Evans" to determine what she was saying about Sarah Drew. Grills also testified that midway through the ruse, Lori Drew changed the plan and wanted to print out copies of Megan's correspondence with "Josh" and confront her with them in public to humiliate her. Sarah Drew said this was discussed at the dinner table one night but it was never a serious plan.

Given the jurors' decision, it appears they believed Sarah Drew's assertion.

Defense attorney Steward indicated he would be seeking a new trial on the three counts but would not do so until after Judge George Wu ruled on a motion for acquittal that Steward filed last Friday. Wu told both sides on Wednesday that he still needed time "to digest" the facts in the case before ruling on the motion. Drew remains out on bond and will have to appear in court for a hearing on December 29th.

O'Brien said he made the decision to prosecute after learning about Drew's crimes from media stories, and he stood by his controversial interpretation of the

Computer Fraud and Abuse Act, an anti-hacking law. He said his office embraced the challenges it faced in being the first to wield the statute in this novel manner.

"I'm comfortable with the decision to indict," O'Brien said.

Thomas Mrozek, spokesman for the U.S. Attorney's Office in Los Angeles, told Threat Level that the office's cybercrime and intellectual property unit examined the laws to determine what charges might be filed against Drew, and determined that the Computer Fraud and Abuse Act was the most appropriate. Mrozek said there was no opposition in their office to bringing the charges.

Asked why he took the unusual step of prosecuting the case himself instead of passing it off to assistant U.S. attorneys, O'Brien said the case "means a lot to me," adding, "you can't help but be touched by the tragedy."

He also said that the indictment sent a message that "if you are going to ... go after a little girl, this office as well as other U.S. attorney offices, will do anything possible to go after you."

He added that he was "astounded by some of the comments I read, that people think they can do whatever they want on the internet." He said the case was a warning to parents that if they're not watching what their kids are doing online, "you better be."

Tina Meier said she was grateful to the U.S. attorney's office that it had "stepped up and done an amazing job."

She insisted that the case had "never been about vengeance," but about justice, and about helping prevent similar tragedies from happening again.

Asked if it was hard to sit through the case and hear the verdict, Meier replied, "This day is not any harder than it was the day I found Megan."

Drew's attorney, Steward, said that although most lawyers would welcome the lesser misdemeanor convictions, he and his client felt "no joy" in it, due to the tragic nature of the case. "Everyone feels the pain of the Meiers," he said.

In responding to a question about why his client showed no emotion throughout the trial, even when her daughter Sarah broke down on the stand twice, he said Drew had been under assault on the internet and in real life, and that she had developed defenses.

"That's why you didn't see a lot of crying or emotion," he said.

One puzzling aspect of the verdict, Steward said, was how the jury managed to agree that Drew was guilty of misdemeanor computer intrusions, but remained deadlocked on the charge of conspiracy to commit that intrusion, since the charges were all closely related.

He said the misdemeanor convictions sent a mixed message. If there had been a felony conviction, computer users would have to be concerned that they might be charged with a felony for violating a web site's terms of service. But the misdemeanor conviction, he said, "deflects that."

Writing on his blog, former Justice Department computer crime prosecutor Orin Kerr, who helped defend Drew, said he was waiting for the judge to rule on the motion for acquittal. If the convictions are upheld, he anticipates an appeal.

Cyberspace Threats and Vulnerabilities[*]

Excerpted from *The National Strategy to Secure Cyberspace*
U.S. Department of Homeland Security, February 2003

A CASE FOR ACTION

The terrorist attacks against the United States that took place on September 11, 2001, had a profound impact on our Nation. The federal government and society as a whole have been forced to reexamine conceptions of security on our home soil, with many understanding only for the first time the lengths to which self-designated enemies of our country are willing to go to inflict debilitating damage.

We must move forward with the understanding that there are enemies who seek to inflict damage on our way of life. They are ready to attack us on our own soil, and they have shown a willingness to use unconventional means to execute those attacks. While the attacks of September 11 were physical attacks, we are facing increasing threats from hostile adversaries in the realm of cyberspace as well.

A NATION NOW FULLY DEPENDENT ON CYBERSPACE

For the United States, the information technology revolution quietly changed the way business and government operate. Without a great deal of thought about security, the Nation shifted the control of essential processes in manufacturing, utilities, banking, and communications to networked computers. As a result, the cost of doing business dropped and productivity skyrocketed. The trend toward greater use of networked systems continues.

By 2003, our economy and national security became fully dependent upon information technology and the information infrastructure. A network of networks directly supports the operation of all sectors of our economy—energy (electric

* Published by the U.S. Department of Homeland Security, February 2003.

power, oil and gas), transportation (rail, air, merchant marine), finance and banking, information and telecommunications, public health, emergency services, water, chemical, defense industrial base, food, agriculture, and postal and shipping. The reach of these computer networks exceeds the bounds of cyberspace. They also control physical objects such as electrical transformers, trains, pipeline pumps, chemical vats, and radars.

THREATS IN CYBERSPACE

A spectrum of malicious actors can and do conduct attacks against our critical information infrastructures. Of primary concern is the threat of organized cyber attacks capable of causing debilitating disruption to our Nation's critical infrastructures, economy, or national security. The required technical sophistication to carry out such an attack is high—and partially explains the lack of a debilitating attack to date. We should not, however, be too sanguine. There have been instances where attackers have exploited vulnerabilities that may be indicative of more destructive capabilities.

Uncertainties exist as to the intent and full technical capabilities of several observed attacks. Enhanced cyber threat analysis is needed to address long-term trends related to threats and vulnerabilities. What is known is that the attack tools and methodologies are becoming widely available, and the technical capability and sophistication of users bent on causing havoc or disruption is improving. As an example, consider the "NIMDA" ("ADMIN" spelled backwards) attack. Despite the fact that NIMDA did not create a catastrophic disruption to the critical infrastructure, it is a good example of the increased technical sophistication showing up in cyber attacks. It demonstrated that the arsenal of weapons available to organized attackers now contains the capability to learn and adapt to its local environment. NIMDA was an automated cyber attack, a blend of a computer worm and a computer virus. It propagated across the Nation with enormous speed and tried several different ways to infect computer systems it invaded until it gained access and destroyed files. It went from nonexistent to nationwide in an hour, lasted for days, and attacked 86,000 computers. Speed is also increasing. Consider that two months before NIMDA, a cyber attack called Code Red infected 150,000 computer systems in 14 hours.

Because of the increasing sophistication of computer attack tools, an increasing number of actors are capable of launching nationally significant assaults against our infrastructures and cyberspace. In peacetime America's enemies may conduct espionage on our Government, university research centers, and private companies. They may also seek to prepare for cyber strikes during a confrontation by mapping U.S. information systems, identifying key targets, lacing our infrastructure with back doors and other means of access. In wartime or crisis, adversaries may seek to intimidate the nation's political leaders by attacking critical infrastructures and key economic functions or eroding public confidence in information systems.

Cyber attacks on U.S. information networks can have serious consequences such as disrupting critical operations, causing loss of revenue and intellectual property, or loss of life. Countering such attacks requires the development of robust capabilities where they do not exist today if we are to reduce vulnerabilities and deter those with the capabilities and intent to harm our critical infrastructures.

Cyberspace provides a means for organized attack on our infrastructure from a distance. These attacks require only commodity technology, and enable attackers to obfuscate their identities, locations, and paths of entry. Not only does cyberspace provide the ability to exploit weaknesses in our critical infrastructures, but it also provides a fulcrum for leveraging physical attacks by allowing the possibility of disrupting communications, hindering U.S. defensive or offensive response, or delaying emergency responders who would be essential following a physical attack.

In the last century, geographic isolation helped protect the United States from a direct physical invasion. In cyberspace national boundaries have little meaning. Information flows continuously and seamlessly across political, ethnic, and religious divides. Even the infrastructure that makes up cyberspace—software and hardware—is global in its design and development. Because of the global nature of cyberspace, the vulnerabilities that exist are open to the world and available to anyone, anywhere, with sufficient capability to exploit them.

REDUCE VULNERABILITIES IN THE ABSENCE OF KNOWN THREATS

While the Nation's critical infrastructures must, of course, deal with specific threats as they arise, waiting to learn of an imminent attack before addressing important critical infrastructure vulnerabilities is a risky and unacceptable strategy. Cyber attacks can burst onto the Nation's networks with little or no warning and spread so fast that many victims never have a chance to hear the alarms. Even with forewarning, they likely would not have had the time, knowledge, or tools needed to protect themselves. In some cases creating defenses against these attacks would have taken days.

A key lesson derived from these and other such cyber attacks is that organizations that rely on networked computer systems must take proactive steps to identify and remedy their vulnerabilities, rather than waiting for an attacker to be stopped or until alerted of an impending attack. Vulnerability assessment and remediation activities must be ongoing. An information technology security audit conducted by trained professionals to identify infrastructure vulnerabilities can take months. Subsequently, the process of creating a multilayered defense and a resilient network to remedy the most serious vulnerabilities could take several additional months. The process must then be regularly repeated.

THREAT AND VULNERABILITY: A FIVE-LEVEL PROBLEM

Managing threat and reducing vulnerability in cyberspace is a particularly complex challenge because of the number and range of different types of users. Cyberspace security requires action on multiple levels and by a diverse group of actors because literally hundreds of millions of devices are interconnected by a network of networks. The problem of cyberspace security can be best addressed on five levels.

Level 1, the Home User/Small Business

Though not a part of a critical infrastructure the computers of home users can become part of networks of remotely controlled machines that are then used to attack critical infrastructures. Undefended home and small business computers, particularly those using digital subscriber line (DSL) or cable connections, are vulnerable to attackers who can employ the use of those machines without the owner's knowledge. Groups of such "zombie" machines can then be used by third-party actors to launch denial-of-service (DoS) attacks on key Internet nodes and other important enterprises or critical infrastructures.

Level 2, Large Enterprises

Large-scale enterprises (corporations, government agencies, and universities) are common targets for cyber attacks. Many such enterprises are part of critical infrastructures. Enterprises require clearly articulated, active information security policies and programs to audit compliance with cybersecurity best practices. According to the U.S. intelligence community, American networks will be increasingly targeted by malicious actors both for the data and the power they possess.

Level 3, Critical Sectors/Infrastructures

When organizations in sectors of the economy, government, or academia unite to address common cybersecurity problems, they can often reduce the burden on individual enterprises. Such collaboration often produces shared institutions and mechanisms, which, in turn, could have cyber vulnerabilities whose exploitation could directly affect the operations of member enterprises and the sector as a whole.

Enterprises can also reduce cyber risks by participating in groups that develop best practices, evaluate technological offerings, certify products and services, and share information. Several sectors have formed Information Sharing and Analysis Centers (ISACs) to monitor for cyber attacks directed against their respective infrastructures. ISACs are also a vehicle for sharing information about attack trends, vulnerabilities, and best practices.

Level 4, National Issues and Vulnerabilities

Some cybersecurity problems have national implications and cannot be solved by individual enterprises or infrastructure sectors alone. All sectors share the Internet. Accordingly, they are all at risk if its mechanisms (e.g., protocols and routers) are not secure. Weaknesses in widely used software and hardware products can also create problems at the national level, requiring coordinated activities for the research and development of improved technologies.

Additionally, the lack of trained and certified cybersecurity professionals also merits national level concern.

Level 5, Global

The worldwide web is a planetary information grid of systems. Internationally shared standards enable interoperability among the world's computer systems. This interconnectedness, however, also means that problems on one continent have the potential to affect computers on another. We therefore rely on international cooperation to share information related to cyber issues and, further, to prosecute cyber criminals. Without such cooperation, our collective ability to detect, deter, and minimize the effects of cyber-based attacks would be greatly diminished.

NEW VULNERABILITIES REQUIRING CONTINUOUS RESPONSE

New vulnerabilities are created or discovered regularly. The process of securing networks and systems, therefore, must also be continuous. The Computer Emergency Response Team/Coordination Center (CERT/CC) notes that not only are the numbers of cyber incidents and attacks increasing at an alarming rate, so too are the numbers of vulnerabilities that an attacker could exploit. Identified computer security vulnerabilities—faults in software and hardware that could permit unauthorized network access or allow an attacker to cause network damage—increased significantly from 2000 to 2002, with the number of vulnerabilities going from 1,090 to 4,129.

The mere installation of a network security device is not a substitute for maintaining and updating a network's defenses. Ninety percent of the participants in a recent Computer Security Institute survey reported using antivirus software on their network systems, yet 85 percent of their systems had been damaged by computer viruses. In the same survey, 89 percent of the respondents had installed computer firewalls, and 60 percent had intrusion detection systems. Nevertheless, 90 percent reported that security breaches had taken place, and 40 percent of their systems had been penetrated from outside their network. The majority of security vulnerabilities can be mitigated through good security practices. As these survey numbers indicate, however, practicing good security includes more than simply installing those devices. It also requires operating them correctly and keeping them current through regular patching and virus updates.

CYBERSECURITY AND OPPORTUNITY COST

For individual companies and the national economy as a whole, improving computer security requires investing attention, time, and money. For fiscal year 2003, President Bush requested that Congress increase funds to secure federal computers by 64 percent. President Bush's investment in securing federal computer networks now will eventually reduce overall expenditures through cost-saving E-Government solutions, modern enterprise management, and by reducing the number of opportunities for waste and fraud. For the national economy—particularly its information technology industry component—the dearth of trusted, reliable, secure information systems presents a barrier to future growth. Much of the potential for economic growth made possible by the information technology revolution has yet to be realized—deterred in part by cyberspace security risks. Cyberspace vulnerabilities place more than transactions at risk; they jeopardize intellectual property, business operations, infrastructure services, and consumer trust. Conversely, cybersecurity investments result in more than costly overhead expenditures. They produce a return on investment. Surveys repeatedly show that:

- Although the likelihood of suffering a severe cyber attack is difficult to estimate, the costs associated with a successful one are likely to be greater than the investment in a cybersecurity program to prevent it; and
- Designing strong security protocols into the information systems architecture of an enterprise can reduce its overall operational costs by enabling cost-saving processes, such as remote access and customer or supply-chain interactions, which could not occur in networks lacking appropriate security.

These results suggest that, with greater awareness of the issues, companies can benefit from increasing their levels of cybersecurity. Greater awareness and voluntary efforts are critical components of the *National Strategy to Secure Cyberspace*.

INDIVIDUAL AND NATIONAL RISK MANAGEMENT

Until recently overseas terrorist networks had caused limited damage in the United States. On September 11, 2001, that quickly changed. One estimate places the increase in cost to our economy from attacks to U.S. information systems at 400 percent over four years. While those losses remain relatively limited, that too could change abruptly.

Every day in the United States individual companies, and home computer users, suffer damage from cyber attacks that, to the victims, represent significant losses. Conditions likewise exist for relative measures of damage to occur on a national level, affecting the networks and systems on which the Nation depends:

- Potential adversaries have the intent;
- Tools that support malicious activities are broadly available; and,

- Vulnerabilities of the Nation's systems are many and well known.

No single strategy can completely eliminate cyberspace vulnerabilities and their associated threats. Nevertheless, the Nation must act to manage risk responsibly and to enhance its ability to minimize the damage that results from attacks that do occur. Through this statement, we reveal nothing to potential foes that they and others do not already know. In 1997 a Presidential Commission identified the risks in a seminal public report. In 2000 the first national plan to address the problem was published. Citing these risks, President Bush issued an Executive Order in 2001, making cybersecurity a priority, and accordingly, increasing funds to secure federal networks. In 2002 the President moved to consolidate and strengthen federal cybersecurity agencies as part of the proposed Department of Homeland Security.

GOVERNMENT ALONE CANNOT SECURE CYBERSPACE

Despite increased awareness around the importance of cybersecurity and the measures taken thus far to improve our capabilities, cyber risks continue to underlie our national information networks and the critical systems they manage. Reducing that risk requires an unprecedented, active partnership among diverse components of our country and our global partners.

The federal government could not—and, indeed, should not—secure the computer networks of privately owned banks, energy companies, transportation firms, and other parts of the private sector. The federal government should likewise not intrude into homes and small businesses, into universities, or state and local agencies and departments to create secure computer networks. Each American who depends on cyberspace, the network of information networks, must secure the part that they own or for which they are responsible.

National Policy and Guiding Principles[*]

Excerpted from *The National Strategy to Secure Cyberspace*
U.S. Department of Homeland Security, February 2003

NATIONAL POLICY, PRINCIPLES, AND ORGANIZATION

This section describes the national policy that shapes the National Strategy to Secure Cyberspace and the basic framework of principles within which it was developed. It also outlines the roles and missions of federal agencies.

NATIONAL POLICY

The information technology revolution has changed the way business is transacted, government operates, and national defense is conducted. These three functions now depend on an interdependent network of critical information infrastructures that we refer to as "cyberspace."

It is the policy of the United States to prevent or minimize disruptions to critical information infrastructures and thereby protect the people, the economy, the essential human and government services, and the national security of the United States. Disruptions that do occur should be infrequent, of minimal duration and manageable and cause the least damage possible. The policy requires a continuous effort to secure information systems for critical infrastructure and includes voluntary public-private partnerships involving corporate and nongovernmental organizations.

Consistent with the objectives of the *National Strategy for Homeland Security*, the objectives of the *National Strategy to Secure Cyberspace* are to:
- Prevent cyber attacks against our critical infrastructures;
- Reduce our national vulnerabilities to cyber attack; and,

---

[*] Published by the U.S. Department of Homeland Security, February 2003.

- Minimize the damage and recovery time from cyber attacks that do occur. Guiding Principles In January 2001, the Administration began to review the role of information systems and cybersecurity. In October 2001, President Bush issued Executive Order 13231, authorizing a protection program that consists of continuous efforts to secure information systems for critical infrastructure, including emergency preparedness communications and the physical assets that support such systems. The Federal Information Security Management Act (FISMA) and Executive Order 13231, together with other relevant Presidential directives and statutory authorities, provide the framework for executive branch cyberspace security activities.

The protection of these cyber systems is essential to every sector of the economy. The development and implementation of this program directive has been guided by the following organizing principles:

1. *A National Effort:* Protecting the widely distributed assets of cyberspace requires the efforts of many Americans. The federal government alone cannot defend America's cyberspace. Our traditions of federalism and limited government require that organizations outside the federal government take the lead in many of these efforts. The government's role in securing cyberspace includes promoting better security in privately owned infrastructures when there is a need to:

- Convene and facilitate discussions between and with nongovernmental entities;
- Identify instances where the "tragedy of the commons" can affect homeland, national, and economic security; and
- Share information about cyber threats and vulnerabilities so nongovernmental entities can adjust their risk management strategies and plans, as appropriate.

In every case, the scope for government involvement is limited to those cases when the benefits of intervention outweigh the direct and indirect costs.

Every American who can contribute to securing part of cyberspace is encouraged to do so. The federal government promotes the creation of, and participation in, public-private partnerships to raise awareness, train personnel, stimulate market forces, improve technology, identify and remediate vulnerabilities, exchange information, and plan recovery operations. Many sectors have undertaken the important step of developing ISACs, which facilitate communication, the development of best practices, and the dissemination of security-related information. In addition, various sectors have developed plans to secure their parts of cyberspace, which complement this *Strategy*, and the government intends for this productive and collaborative partnership to continue.

2. *Protect Privacy and Civil Liberties:* The abuse of cyberspace infringes on our privacy and our liberty. It is incumbent on the federal government to avoid such abuse and infringement. Cybersecurity and personal privacy need not be opposing goals. Cyberspace security programs must strengthen, not weaken, such protections. Accordingly, care must be taken to respect privacy interests and other civil

liberties. Consumers and operators must have confidence their voluntarily shared, nonpublic information will be handled accurately, confidentially, and reliably. The federal government will lead by example in implementing strong privacy policies and practices in the agencies. As part of this process, the federal government will consult regularly with privacy advocates and experts.

3. *Regulation and Market Forces:* federal regulation will not become a primary means of securing cyberspace. Broad regulations mandating how all corporations must configure their information systems could divert more successful efforts by creating a lowest-common denominator approach to cybersecurity, which evolving technology would quickly marginalize. Even worse, such an approach could result in less secure and more homogeneous security architectures than we have now. By law, some federal regulatory agencies already include cybersecurity considerations in their oversight activity. However, the market itself is expected to provide the major impetus to improve cybersecurity.

4. *Accountability and Responsibility:* The *National Strategy to Secure Cyberspace* is focused on producing a more resilient and reliable information infrastructure. When possible, it designates lead executive branch departments or agencies for federal cyberspace security initiatives. On November 25, 2002, the President signed the *Homeland Security Act of 2002* establishing the Department of Homeland Security (DHS). DHS will be responsible for many of the initiatives outlined in the *National Strategy to Secure Cyberspace.* The *Strategy* also recommends actions federal, state and local governments, the private sector, and the American people can take to help secure cyberspace.

5. *Ensure Flexibility:* Cyber threats change rapidly. Accordingly, the *National Strategy to Secure Cyberspace* emphasizes flexibility in our ability to respond to cyber attacks and manage vulnerability reduction. The rapid development of attack tools provides potential attackers with a strategic advantage to adapt their offensive tactics quickly to target perceived weaknesses in networked information systems and organizations' abilities to respond. Flexible planning allows organizations to reassess priorities and realign resources as the cyber threat evolves.

6. *Multi-Year Planning:* Securing cyberspace is an ongoing process, as new technologies appear and new vulnerabilities are identified. The *National Strategy to Secure Cyberspace* provides an initial framework for achieving cyberspace security objectives. Departments and agencies should adopt multi-year cybersecurity plans for sustaining their respective roles. Other public- and private-sector organizations are also encouraged to consider multi-year plans.

DEPARTMENT OF HOMELAND SECURITY AND CYBERSPACE SECURITY

DHS unites 22 federal entities for the common purpose of improving homeland security. The Department also creates a focal point for managing cyberspace incidents that could impact the federal government or even the national information infrastructures. The Secretary of Homeland Security will have important responsibilities in cyberspace security, including:

- Developing a comprehensive national plan for securing the key resources and critical infrastructures of the United States, including information technology and telecommunications systems (including satellites) and the physical and technological assets that support such systems;
- Providing crisis management support in response to threats to, or attacks on, critical information systems;
- Providing technical assistance to the private sector and other governmental entities with respect to emergency recovery plans that respond to major failures of critical information systems;
- Coordinating with other federal agencies to provide specific warning information and advice about appropriate protective measures and countermeasures to state and local government agencies and authorities, the private sector, other entities, and the public; and
- Performing and funding research and development along with other agencies that will lead to new scientific understanding and technologies in support of homeland security.

DESIGNATION OF COORDINATING AGENCIES

A productive partnership between the federal government and the private sector depends on effective coordination and communication. To facilitate and enhance this collaborative structure, the government has designated a "Lead Agency" for each of the major sectors of the economy vulnerable to infrastructure attack. In addition, the Office of Science and Technology Policy (OSTP) coordinates research and development to support critical infrastructure protection. The Office of Management and Budget (OMB) oversees the implementation of governmentwide policies, principles, standards, and guidelines for federal government computer security programs. The Department of State coordinates international outreach on cybersecurity. The Director of Central Intelligence is responsible for assessing the foreign threat to U.S. networks and information systems. The Department of Justice (DOJ) and the Federal Bureau of Investigation (FBI) lead the national effort to investigate and prosecute cybercrime.

The government will continue to support the development of public-private partnerships. Working together, sector representatives and federal lead agencies assess their respective sectors' vulnerabilities to cyber or physical attacks and, accordingly, recommend plans or measures to eliminate significant exposures. Both technology and the threat environment can change rapidly. Therefore, sectors and lead agencies should frequently assess the reliability, vulnerability, and threat environments of the Nation's infrastructures and employ appropriate protective measures and responses to safeguard them.

The government's full authority, capabilities, and resources must be available to support critical infrastructure protection efforts. These include, as appropriate, crisis management, law enforcement, regulation, foreign intelligence, and defense preparedness.

2

Viruses, Spam, and NetBots

Editor's Introduction

The virus is perhaps the best-known form of computer threat. A virus can replicate itself and infect computers without the knowledge or permission of users. Each year, consumers, businesses, governments, and other institutions invest heavily in purchasing and updating anti-virus software. Still, as anti-virus measures become more sophisticated, so too do the viruses themselves. Consequently, even the most up-to-date safeguards are not foolproof and are effective only for as long it takes someone to locate their flaws and devise ways to exploit them.

Among the other drawbacks of the digital age is the spam e-mail. These unwanted solicitations and advertisements, peddling anything from anabolic steroids to pornography, have become ever present and an accepted fact of life for just about anyone with an e-mail account. Often looked on as a mere annoyance, resulting in little more than a clogged inbox, spam can have more sinister implications: spam e-mails sometimes have viruses embedded in them; others attempt to fool people into giving out personal information, in a trick known as "phishing," which can potentially result in identity theft and worse.

Another threat that has developed is the botnet. Botnets are networks of "zombie" or robot computers. Compromised by a virus, these computers are effectively taken over by a "bot herder," who then uses them to generate spam e-mails or viruses, to install spyware, or for other nefarious purposes. Often the owner has no idea his or her computer has been commandeered. Some of these botnets have employed hundreds of thousands of zombie computers.

This chapter focuses on the three aforementioned types of attacks. In the first article, "Malware, Spyware, Spamware, Beware," Yan Barcelo explains how technological advances have created a need for increased security. In addition to computers, many new products—everything from flash cards to electronic picture frames—require protection. Barcelo discusses how to protect oneself from these attacks, as well as what to do when a computer or device is infected.

In the next piece, "Beware the Digital Zombies," John Markoff explores how computers can be taken over by botnets and incorporated into systems of computer that have also been overtaken. Markoff examines Microsoft's efforts to counter botnets, since that company's operating system and software are frequently the target.

"Bugging Broadband," by Charles Arthur, describes security threats in Great Britain, where computers with broadband Internet connections have become repositories for viruses, Trojan horses, worms, and other dangerous software.

Most of these threats are directed at personal computers, or PCs, which are employed by the overwhelming majority of computer users. This has led many who work with Apple Inc.'s Macintosh, or Mac, computers to assume they remain safe. This assumption is further reinforced by Macintosh's reputation for security and user-friendliness. However, as Seth Colaner explains in "A Slice of Apple: Mac Attacks!," using a Macintosh is not a panacea against computer viruses and the like, and consequently Mac users need to take steps to ensure their machines remain secure.

Malware, Spyware, Spamware, Beware[*]

By Yan Barcelo
CA Magazine, September 2008

Threats abound in cyberspace and their numbers are increasing exponentially.

Yet cyberspace is only one corner—albeit a big one—of the information universe.

Security has to do with not only the Excel file you carry around in your laptop computer but also with the financial report you hold in your desk drawer. And what about that fellow on the maintenance team who has access to the computer room after hours? In the information age, key security software does not reside in your employees' computers, but in their heads. You could call it "beware."

Yesterday, information could only be stolen. Today, not only can it be stolen, it can be compromised, corrupted, intercepted, lost and quarantined. Let us count the ways.

THROUGH THE SIDE DOOR

At one time PCs were the only digital thing people had to worry about. Today, one has to worry about peripheral devices whose numbers and diversity increase by leaps and bounds, says Yves Godbout, director of IT services at the Office of the Auditor General of Canada in Ottawa (and *CA Magazine*'s technical editor for Technology).

Who would have suspected that digital photo frames could be dangerous? But that's what people who bought such cute devices recently discovered. Thousands of digital frames were taken out of circulation in the US after clients who connected their PC to the device discovered they had uploaded a variant of the Mocmex virus—dubbed the nuclear bomb of viruses—that blocked the antivirus and firewall software of more than 100 suppliers and automatically downloaded infected files from an IP address and renamed these randomly to make their retracing nearly impossible. "Experts asked if it was an attempt by Chinese manufacturers to spy or carry out infiltration tests on Western computer networks," says Benoit Gagnon, associate researcher at the Canada Research Chair in security, identity and technology at Université de Montréal.

USB keys, easily lost or stolen, are another growing headache. Since the devices are minuscule, people tend to be negligent with them. "Yet a single USB key with one gigabyte of capacity can contain as much information as the hard disks of a mainframe of 25 years ago that was guarded behind steel-reinforced doors," says Godbout. USB keys are excellent contamination vehicles: plugged into a computer, they can pick up countless viruses and malware that, once transferred to the office PC, can spread through the corporate network.

The same goes for CDs and DVDs with their massive storage and backup capacity. They have become so ubiquitous that people forget they can contain sensitive data. Unfortunately, the same security measures that apply to usual storage devices are not necessarily followed through on these devices and they often circulate unprotected, Godbout says.

Intelligent phones, iPhones and personal digital assistants are another hot growth area that hackers and criminals increasingly target. The United States Computer Emergency Readiness Team recently reported a Trojan worm that infected mobile phones running the SymbianOS operating system and propagated itself to other phones by sending malicious files to the contacts listed in an infected device.

Contamination is not the only problem with mobile devices. People discuss many sensitive things over their Bluetooth-enabled mobile phones. "If I wanted to do industrial espionage, all I would need to do is walk around hotel corridors with a device to pick up Bluetooth or WiFi communications," says Gagnon.

THE FRONT DOOR

Of course, threats have not all migrated to peripherals. PCs are still targets of choice. Everyone knows how unprotected machines can be bogged down or hard disks destroyed by viruses, and companies increasingly make sure all entrance doors are locked. But what about the exit doors? What about discarded PCs whose hard disks have not been thoroughly wiped clean that end up on a competitor's desk? Yet a simple little utility, priced between $29 and $89, will do the job.

And what about the countless hours people spend surfing the Net? In offices, employees connect to peer-to-peer networks where they expose their companies to all kinds of damage and malware. Only two years ago, websites were relatively safe places, built from static pages a surfer could only consult. Now, with the Web 2.0 wave moving across the Internet, sites are interactive: you click on a button, an image or a banner and bingo, you have downloaded adware, spyware or a virus.

In fact, it is worse than that. "Today, simply by navigating on a website you can be contaminated without even downloading anything," says Jacques Viau, director of the Information Security Institute of Quebec. And don't think all such sites are the seedy XXX type. "More than 50% of these are legitimate corporate sites that have been unknowingly contaminated because of vulnerabilities and defects in their software coding," says Viau.

Such contaminations are usually the work of botnets, which are vast networks of tens of thousands of PCs enslaved unbeknownst to their owners by hackers. These slaves are programmed by their botmasters to broadcast malware (spyware, adware, viruses, phishing, keyloggers, etc.) to hundreds of thousands of other PCs. According to Sam Norris, president of ChangeIP.com, in a 2006 Washington Post article, authorities are starting to understand that botnets are the source of all evil on the Internet today, from hacking and spamming to phishing and spying.

The first problem with a botnet is having a PC or server enslaved to one. If you think this is the reserved province of hijacked home computers, think again. Norris discovered a ring of 10,000 infected PCs inside a Fortune 100 company that the network administrator had no idea what to do about.

But the really dirty part of botnets is what they do with PCs and their owners. One botnet program Norris dissected contained instructions to install 14 adware and spyware programs that none of the antivirus software he uses was able to detect. Once executed, these malwares did things such as run pornographic pop-up ads or install an XXX site toolbar in Explorer. More severe threats came from instructions designed to capture the victim's Web activities, or keystrokes, even peer through his or her webcam. But the real damage came from a small program that took passwords and credentials the victim uses to log into online accounts at PayPal, eBay, Bank of America, Citibank and others.

SOFTWARE—VERY SOFT

In the war to compromise, steal or alter information, the Internet is a major vector, but not the only one. In fact, the foremost one has nothing to do with websites, USB keys or digital frames; it has to do with people, the softer part of software. "All the reports say most security breaches are committed internally by employees," Godbout says. Of course, such breaches can be intentional, as when a disgruntled or fired employee plants a virus in the corporate network. Or when an employee deliberately steals information to sell it to a competitor.

But most breaches are unintentional and perpetrated by employees who are negligent with their passwords, DVDs, mobile phones or iPods. Well-meaning employees can be helpful over the phone to anonymous callers asking the whereabouts of executives or clients. "Secretaries are a privileged target of social engineers," says Gagnon. "They are paid to be nice and helpful. They're often overworked, so security issues are not a priority."

Gagnon tested a facility where access was controlled by two tough hardware measures: a magnetic card and a fingerprint reader. Appearing as a delivery man carrying two boxes, he beamed an embarrassed smile and an employee let him in and politely gave directions.

Another channel by which information can be squandered and lost is the one companies open with subcontractors, offshore manufacturers and outside experts. Sensitive data and corporate information can be handed over to these external players whose discretion is not guaranteed. "One has to question whether the game is worth the security risk," Gagnon says. "Especially since information is increasingly what the game is about. It brings into question the fundamental corporate strategy of the past 10 years of keeping only core activities and outsourcing the rest."

Gagnon points to a robotics startup company that shared parts of its invention with a subcontractor only to find later that another company beat it to the market with the same invention. "It would have been better off paying high salaries to hired specialists and paying itself back with its invention's sales," he says.

EVERYMAN'S SECURITY

Security is now seen as synonymous with computer security. But it is much larger and has to do with information and anything that carries that information: computers, hard-disk drives, filing cabinets, buildings and people—especially people.

That is why the cardinal rule of security concerns people and their training. "Employee training is 50% of the security recipe," Viau says. "One negligent employee can compromise with a single gesture the security a company has built with millions invested in hardware and software. We always think we have done enough training. It is not the case. We often end up lowering our guard." It is not a question of being paranoid, says Viau. That risks compromising the relationship a company has with its employees and, ultimately, with clients. But a healthy dose of prudence is called for.

That is why a corporation's security plan starts at the highest level—in the board room and at the CEO's desk—with well-articulated policies and rules. But it is not enough to state rules. Employees must be made aware of the dangers that threaten information in all its guises, risky behaviours must be illustrated through concrete examples, their consequences explained and the right correctives and attitudes demonstrated.

The importance of security training became transparent to SNC-Lavalin. "We came to realize that even though we put countless technological solutions in place, humans remained the weak link," says Denis Normand, manager of computer security at the engineering firm.

SNC-Lavalin's security needs are particularly acute but nevertheless emblematic of a situation that is prevalent in an increasing number of companies involved globally. His firm, says Normand, is involved in many international collaborative projects, often with competitors, carried out over computer networks or through direct personal interaction. Exchanges take place globally through mobile devices over communications infrastructures of unequal quality and security levels. In such a context, a slight indiscretion or a temporary lack of vigilance can have regrettable consequences. And it is impossible to secure all transactions through hardware and software alone. Employees, above all, must beware.

To some extent, a company must also be aware of its employees, a little more of its subcontractors and outside collaborators. When recruiting, internally or externally, a security check is always necessary. When terminating, all access privileges and passwords must be cancelled immediately. Large corporations go through these procedures routinely, but small and medium-sized companies fall short of such measures.

Of course, software and hardware are also part of the security equation. And a number of interventions are proposed by the Internet Security Alliance.

SOFTWARE CONTROLS

Install all necessary protection software: antivirus, antispyware, antispam, firewall—Do not simply base your choice on name and reputation. Symantec's utilities have a big signature in the market, but are not the best buy. In March 2008, AV-Test GmbH tested antivirus programs against 1.13 million known malware samples. Products such as Secure Computing's Webwasher and G Data's Total Care showed detection levels of 99.9%, while Symantec's and MacAfee's were only 95.6% and 95.7% respectively. On such a sample, that means Symantec and MacAfee let approximately 49,000 malwares go by.

Keep current with software updates—Even though updates can create havoc, they are imperative. Such was the case at the Royal Bank in 2004 when some databases were corrupted, causing several clients to lose access to their accounts and preventing them from applying transactions to their accounts for a few days. Afterward, the bank implemented a rigid and structured change management process for all application changes. When asked if the bank followed the same rigorous steps for security updates, such as Microsoft updates, as for application changes, the manager responsible for change management at RBC Financial Group said that after a review, the bank came up with the following conclusion: the risk of implementing an upgrade too quickly was less than the problems created by not implementing it.

Such updates concern all major programs a company works with (operating systems, productivity applications, security programs), especially utilities used in downloading material from the Web (Adobe Acrobat, Winzip, RealPlayer, etc.). Increasingly, hackers exploit vulnerabilities in these secondary applications to gain access to corporate systems.

Use strong access controllers—Passwords are the most prevalent form of access control; they should be as complex as users will be able to remember and changed regularly. But stronger devices should be used wherever the company can afford them: dynamic password generators, biometric readers, mostly for fingerprints.

Establish physical access controls to all premises, especially to computer equipment—Do not be content with symbolic security measures, for example simply putting a lock on a door, but ensure the door frame is solidly anchored. Do not lose sight of the forest because of the trees; for example, a company houses its main computer systems in a well-secured room—but against an exterior wall.

Prepare a continuity plan—Imagine going through a major breakdown or catastrophe (fire, flood, terrorist attack, etc.). Then answer the question, what do you need to put in place to make sure the event does not drive you into bankruptcy: file and software backups, redundant systems, available office space, identification of key personnel?

Last piece of advice—beware.

WHO YOU GONNA CALL?

When data gets corrupted or when a competitor brings to market a product you have been working on for two years, who are you going to call to complain? Assigning responsibility for information risk is more art than science.

For example, it may not be a good idea to make the IT director responsible for system audits. Even if he or she is honest, the director could have a tendency to downplay vulnerabilities in an area he or she has neglected. It may be better to have a security officer report to the CFO rather than to the CIO.

Also, as information security is a larger domain than information system security, it may be relevant to have the CIO and the chief information security officer (CISO) report separately to the CEO.

"It all depends on what value a company assigns to its information assets," says Jacques Laporte, manager of consulting services at CGI Group. "A bank or corporation where information value is very high will tend to place a CISO on the same hierarchical level as the CIO, directly under the CEO. In a construction company where the key assets are in the field, not in the offices, a CIO can very well handle all information security needs."

TRANSLATING INFORMATION RISK TO FINANCIAL RISK

Security is a vast and unwieldy domain. "It is impossible to do everything," says Mario Dallaire, senior consultant with CGI Group in Montreal. Prioritizing is essential, and that is why the first phase of a security program is to carry out an information risk assessment.

This assessment rests on two prerequisites, knowing what information assets belong to the company (patents, development plans, client data, supply-chain transactions, etc.) and who the owners of these assets are. This can be a tricky exercise, as CGI Group consulting manager Jacques Laporte explains. "Some owners don't really want this ownership," he says, "and will say that this info belongs to the IT department, which in turn will say it doesn't want any part of it, considering it is only a guardian of this info."

Nevertheless, it is the owners who can really say how crucial their information assets are to their activity and what it means to be deprived of them because they have been stolen, destroyed or contaminated. A practical way of assigning the level of importance of information assets is to rate them according to three criteria: the probability of an event (piracy, theft, fire, etc.); the vulnerability of specific systems; and the impact that an event can have according to three basic values of information: its availability, its integrity and its confidentiality.

Priority is given to sectors where scores come out highest. For example, where a highly probable event targets a very vulnerable system and can have a major impact on data integrity, that is where security measures would need to be applied first. It is not always possible to assign a dollar value to an event. For example, the day you discover your clients' credit card information is for sale on the Web, you cannot really say what the cost is to your reputation, but can you afford it, asks Dallaire.

Nevertheless, owners should strive, when possible, to estimate consequences in dollars, even if it comes out in approximations such as a risk of $10 million to $25 million in loss. However imprecise, such numbers have the virtue of translating in hard business numbers qualitative information risks that would otherwise remain blurry.

One must also keep in mind that risk is not static, says Laporte, so controls must be in place to keep track of changes after security systems and procedures have been implemented. An example would be of a company that relied on e-mail to deal with suppliers and moves to extranet portal transactions. Suddenly, a new universe of potential threats and catastrophes arises that must be assessed, qualified, quantified and kept at bay.

Beware the Digital Zombies[*]

By John Markoff
The New York Times, October 21, 2008

In a windowless room on Microsoft's campus here [Redmond, Wash.], T. J. Campana, a cybercrime investigator, connects an unprotected computer running an early version of Windows XP to the Internet. In about 30 seconds the computer is "owned."

An automated program lurking on the Internet has remotely taken over the PC and turned it into a "zombie." That computer and other zombie machines are then assembled into systems called "botnets"—home and business PCs that are hooked together into a vast chain of cyber-robots that do the bidding of automated programs to send the majority of e-mail spam, to illegally seek financial information and to install malicious software on still more PCs.

Botnets remain an Internet scourge. Active zombie networks created by a growing criminal underground peaked last month at more than half a million computers, according to shadowserver.org, an organization that tracks botnets. Even though security experts have diminished the botnets to about 300,000 computers, that is still twice the number detected a year ago.

The actual numbers may be far larger; Microsoft investigators, who say they are tracking about 1,000 botnets at any given time, say the largest network still controls several million PCs.

"The mean time to infection is less than five minutes," said Richie Lai, who is part of Microsoft's Internet Safety Enforcement Team, a group of about 20 researchers and investigators. The team is tackling a menace that in the last five years has grown from a computer hacker pastime to a dark business that is threatening the commercial viability of the Internet.

Any computer connected to the Internet can be vulnerable. Computer security executives recommend that PC owners run a variety of commercial malware detection programs, like Microsoft's Malicious Software Removal Tool, to find infections of their computers. They should also protect the PCs behind a firewall and install security patches for operating systems and applications.

Even these steps are not a sure thing. Last week Secunia, a computer security firm, said it had tested a dozen leading PC security suites and found that the best one detected only 64 out of 300 software vulnerabilities that make it possible to install malware on a computer.

Botnet attacks now come with their own antivirus software, permitting the programs to take over a computer and then effectively remove other malware competitors. Mr. Campana said the Microsoft investigators were amazed recently to find a botnet that turned on the Microsoft Windows Update feature after taking over a computer, to defend its host from an invasion of competing infections.

Botnets have evolved quickly to make detection more difficult. During the last year botnets began using a technique called fast-flux, which involved generating a rapidly changing set of Internet addresses to make the botnet more difficult to locate and disrupt.

Companies have realized that the only way to combat the menace of botnets and modern computer crime is to build a global alliance that crosses corporate and national boundaries. On Tuesday, Microsoft, the world's largest software company, will convene a gathering of the International Botnet Taskforce in Arlington, Va. At the conference, which is held twice a year, more than 175 members of government and law enforcement agencies, computer security companies and academics will discuss the latest strategies, including legal efforts.

Although the Microsoft team has filed more than 300 civil lawsuits against botnet operators, the company also relies on enforcement agencies like the F.B.I. and Interpol-related organizations for criminal prosecution.

Last month the alliance received support from new federal legislation, which for the first time specifically criminalized the use of botnets. Many of the bots are based in other countries, however, and Mr. Campana said there were many nations with no similar laws.

"It's really a sort of cat-and-mouse situation with the underground," said David Dittrich, a senior security engineer at the University of Washington Applied Physics Laboratory and a member of the International Botnet Taskforce. "Now there's profit motive, and the people doing stuff for profit are doing unique and interesting things."

Microsoft's botnet hunters, who have kept a low profile until now, are led by Richard Boscovich, who until six months ago served as a federal prosecutor in Miami. Mr. Boscovich, a federal prosecutor for 18 years, said he was optimistic that despite the growing number of botnets, progress was being made against computer crime. Recent successes have led to arrests.

"Every time we have a story that says bot-herders get locked up, that helps," said Mr. Boscovich, who in 2000 helped convict Jonathan James, a teenage computer hacker who had gained access to Defense Department and National Air and Space Administration computers.

To aid in its investigations, the Microsoft team has built elaborate software tools including traps called "honeypots" that are used to detect malware and a system called the Botnet Monitoring and Analysis Tool. The software is installed in several refrigerated server rooms on the Microsoft campus that are directly connected to the open Internet, both to mask its location and to make it possible to deploy software sensors around the globe.

The door to the room simply reads "the lab." Inside are racks of hundreds of processors and terabytes of disk drives needed to capture the digital evidence that must be logged as carefully as evidence is maintained by crime scene investigators.

Detecting and disrupting botnets is a particularly delicate challenge that Microsoft will talk about only in vague terms. Their challenge parallels the traditional one of law enforcement's placing informers inside criminal gangs.

Just as gangs will often force a recruit to commit a crime as a test of loyalty, in cyberspace, bot-herders will test recruits in an effort to weed out spies. Microsoft investigators would not discuss their solution to this problem, but said they avoided doing anything illegal with their software.

One possible approach would be to create sensors that would fool the bot-herders by appearing to do malicious things, but in fact not perform the actions.

In 2003 and 2004 Microsoft was deeply shaken by a succession of malicious software worm programs with names like "Blaster" and "Sasser," that raced through the Internet, sowing chaos within corporations and among home computer users. Blaster was a personal affront to the software firm that has long prided itself on its technology prowess. The program contained a hidden message mocking Microsoft's co-founder: "billy gates why do you make this possible? Stop making money and fix your software!!"

The company maintains that its current software is less vulnerable, but even as it fixed some problems, the threat to the world's computers has become far greater. Mr. Campana said that there had been ups and downs in the fight against a new kind of criminal who could hide virtually anywhere in the world and strike with devilish cleverness.

"I come in every morning, and I think we're making progress," he said. At the same time, he said, botnets are not going to go away any time soon.

"There are a lot of very smart people doing very bad things," he said.

Bugging Broadband*

By Charles Arthur
New Statesman, August 29, 2005

The meeting at the Cabinet Office came just after the second set of London bombs, and was attended by the Home Office, police and almost 30 private organisations. They were all gathered, under the grand title of Project Endurance, to consider a desperate question: how do we stop these people? Project Endurance was about to wage war—but not against terrorism. The enemy is another force to which the UK is becoming alarmingly vulnerable: computer viruses.

In the jargon, personal computers harbouring viruses are "compromised". And according to Steve Linford, chief executive of the spam-fighting company Spamhaus, the UK is now "one of the most compromised places in the world". As we in Britain rush to embrace high-speed, always-on internet connections, our computers are turning into repositories for viruses and their nasty friends, worms and "Trojan horse" programs. Linford's company has a "blacklist" of four million internet addresses of computers known to churn out spam. Some are commercial, but many are standard PCs infected by viruses tailored to take over the machine and make it unendingly produce spam, unbeknown to the user. He reckons "hundreds of thousands" of those belong to British internet users, who have unwittingly had their PCs subverted.

This is the problem which led to the July meeting at the Cabinet Office. The participants—including government officials, the National Hi-Tech Crime Unit and dozens of commercial companies such as high-street banks, the auction site eBay, the software giant Microsoft and makers of antivirus software—were trying to work out how to prevent broadband turning into the most widespread computer problem the UK has ever suffered. Project Endurance aims both to educate average users of PCs, and to focus on ways to catch the criminals who steal tens of millions of pounds from Britons every year.

Steve Linford has watched the rising numbers of compromised PCs carefully. In part, he blames the rise of broadband, whose always-on quality gives hackers, viruses and worms unlimited time to attack a machine. A PC on a "dialup" connection can be infected, too, but is less vulnerable because it is not permanently online. It's the difference between a burglar having all day to break in to a secured house, or an hour.

But Linford also blames someone else: Microsoft, whose Windows software powers more than 90 per cent of all personal computers in use. "Nobody likes to say it, but the problem is insecurities in Windows," he says. "The machines we list in our database aren't running Apple or Linux operating systems—they're all Windows. Microsoft really ought to be doing a hell of a lot more to correct the problem."

Microsoft has not been completely indifferent to the internet's abundant threats. Programmers know every piece of software has "bugs". Some are trivial; others can allow hackers to break in to your computer. When Microsoft finds and fixes a crucial bug, it puts a free update online. There's even a setting in Windows that makes PCs seek out such "security patches" and install them automatically. Windows also has a built-in "firewall", which prevents intrusions from outside. But it is only since last September, three years after the introduction of Windows XP, that PCs have been sold with such defences switched on by default. Before that, you'd have to turn them on yourself—if you knew they existed, or were required. And most people don't. Graham Cluley, senior consultant at the PC security company Sophos, says: "People buy computers as consumer items like an LCD TV—but they aren't. With a TV, you just plug it in. A PC is more like a classic car: you have to do tweaks to keep it running perfectly. I really feel sorry for the guys in the street."

Sophos demonstrated just how important such tweaks are last month. It found that if you hook a Windows computer to the internet using a broadband connection, but without any of the protection that professionals use, there is a 50 per cent chance it will be compromised within 12 minutes. That's without user interaction—no web surfing, no e-mail. How? Compromised PCs probe for unpatched machines and infect them in turn. The cycle then repeats.

One might wonder where the harm is. After all, most modern computers have enough spare processor power to churn out some easily ignored spam. However, "malware"—the collective name for the arsenal of programs that infect or subvert PCs—doesn't just use your machine. It watches what you do, so that if you visit particular online banking sites, or type what looks like a credit card number, or a user name and password, these details are recorded and sent silently over the net, using the connection you've paid for, to a remote location. Such "keylogging" was used in Israel recently for industrial espionage.

Then there is the problem of "phishing"—the fake e-mails (sent from compromised machines) saying your online bank account, or eBay or PayPal account, has been suspended or has hosted "suspicious activity". A link in the e-mail directs you to a fake website (often on a compromised PC) where you are encouraged to enter the correct user name and password. These are collected and sent to the hackers. A phishing site running on a compromised broadband PC appears to the user like a real online bank, always available. (With a dial-up connection it would appear and disappear as the user logged on and off the internet. Phishers prefer broadband.) In 2004, £12m was filched from British bank accounts, says Apacs, representing clearing banks in the UK.

Who is behind it all? Nobody is sure, but the evidence points to organised gangs using skilled programmers in the Far East and eastern European countries such as Russia. Yet while Sophos spotted 7,944 new viruses in the first half of 2005, up 59 per cent on the same period last year, none of the perpetrators has been arrested.

This is not how it was meant to be. Broadband was painted as a saviour of British computing, the new white-hot technology that would raise us out of the primeval swamps of the information age and let us stand proud as a knowledge economy. Yet few internet service providers (ISPs) mention that protection of some sort is essential for anyone connecting a personal computer running Windows to a broadband connection.

Brian Aherne, of the Internet Service Providers' Association UK, suggests it is "the punters" who are at fault for not paying enough attention to protecting their PCs with good security software. "We do advise people to get spam filters and firewalls," he insists.

Project Endurance, meanwhile, has made only a slow start. Launched last November by Mike O'Brien, the minister for e-commerce, it came with the promise of an advertising campaign in spring 2005. No, you didn't miss it. The members are still arguing about what to do.

Stephen Millard of the electronic communications security firm MessageLabs is on the project steering group. The problem, he says, is twofold. First, users don't know what to do; and second, they won't want to spend the money and time on antivirus and anti-spyware programs. "Tackling personal responsibility does have costs associated with it," he says. But he likens it to an MOT: "You make sure your car is serviced and has passed an MOT each year." Except that you don't have to keep adding safety features to your car. Millard admits the analogy isn't perfect. "Expectations change," he says. "The level of threat has changed. The ubiquity of the internet has opened up a new channel for people with financial and criminal motivations that we weren't aware of a couple of years ago. People have talked about the advantages of broadband, but they aren't necessarily aware of the implications. The landscape has changed fundamentally."

So does Project Endurance have a clear end point? No, but it might take two or three years to reach a "satisfactory" state. A war whose end point isn't clearly defined and in which the adversaries are shadowy and hard to track down. Sound familiar?

HOW TO PROTECT YOURSELF

- Ensure you have antivirus software. It's never very expensive—some products are even free—and you might find that your computer already came with it.

- Make sure your virus software is kept up to date: This can be automated, and needs updating at least once a week.
- If you have a firewall, turn it on. The latest versions of most operating systems have firewalls built in, but if you're on an older computer, you can obtain firewall software very cheaply—and again, in some cases, free.
- Most importantly, use your common sense. Don't open suspicious e-mails or attachments. Don't click on pop-up adverts. When you're online, remember: if it looks strange, dodgy or too good to be true, it probably is.

A Slice of Apple*

Mac Attacks!

By Seth Colaner
Smart Computing, February 2009

Usually in this column, I talk about applications and hardware that I hope Mac users find useful. This month, we're taking a bit of a deviation from the norm to take a look at the proliferation of Mac malware. For years, Mac users have watched the security train wreck that befalls PCs from a safe distance. Firewalls? Anti-malware? Vulnerabilities in the operating system? These concepts are foreign to those in the Mac camp. And why not? After all, Macs have a stellar record of being virus—and vulnerability—free. However, in recent years there have been more instances of malware targeted at Macs.

AREN'T MACS IMMUNE?

There is some debate as to why exactly Macs have been so virus-free. Some will claim that Macs are designed so well that they are impervious to attack, while others will say that it's simply due to the small market share-meaning that it's not worth a virus-maker's time to create a virus for so few computers when the enormous PC market is ripe for the picking. Still others feel that because Apple started using Intel chips in Macs, the computers will be more vulnerable to PC-like attacks because people are so familiar with the Intel platform. (I'm going to go out on a limb and suggest that this theory doesn't make a great deal of sense and is likely implausible.) Whatever the case may be, Mac users have been incredibly fortunate when it comes to threats from malware.

BENIGN VIRUSES, JUST FOR KICKS

Some people have created harmless "viruses" just to prove the point that Macs can be infected. Granted, these viruses have not-so-subtle ways of getting on your computer—one charming virus actually has to be installed via a special USB flash drive—but you get the gist. It can be done. Personally, I find little humor in these benign viruses. It's like a friend breaking into your house in the middle of the night just to prove that it's possible—you're relieved you aren't being robbed, but it's nevertheless extraordinarily disconcerting.

MALWARE FOR OS X

Though there are few malware programs aimed at Macs, there are a few we should all be aware of.

Backdoor.MacHovdy.a. This Trojan horse is apparently designed to, test a flaw in the ARDAgent (Apple Remote Desktop Agent). Basically, ARDAgent can run Applescript with root privileges. If a user inadvertently installs this little jasper, the hacker has a back door into the user's system. According to a blog post on blog.washingtonpost.com, you can patch this flaw by opening Terminal and entering the following text: osascript -e 'tell app "ARDAgent" to do shell script "chrmod 0555 ISystemlLibrarylCoreServceslRemoteManagementlAR DAgent.app/Contents/MacOS/ARDAgent"'

Keep an eye out for anything resembling ASthtvO5 (a compiled AppleScript), or AStht.y06 (an application bundle), as this is most likely how you'll see the Trojan coming.

OSX.Trojan.PokerStealer. Another recently discovered nasty Trojan, this one will steal your usemame and password and IP (Internet Protocol) addresses. Then the hacker behind it can tear through your computer and even damage the operating system. Fortunately, you can dodge this bullet simply by never downloading anything with the filename PokerGame.app.

Trojan:OSX/DNSChanger. Also known as Trojan: OSX/DNSChanger.A and Trojan:OSX/DNSChanger.C, this Trojan will most likely manifest itself as a fake codec installation when you're trying to view a video. You'll receive a message that you need to get a new version of a codec. Once you click the link and download and install the Trojan, your DNS (Domain Name Server) will point to a malicious Web site. The best protection against this one is vigilance.

DON'T HIDE YOUR MAC UNDER THE MATTRESS

The above is just a sampling of the most recently discovered malware that targets Macs. There are more out there. Yet there's no need to panic—there are bajillions of viruses aimed at PCs and still only a handful for Macs. But the fact remains that as Macs become more beloved and enjoy increased adoption by masses of consumers, hackers and virusmakers will likely devote more time and attention to finding ways to attack them. They're not invincible. It's time for Mac devotees to be more circumspect about security. Remember that even the invincible Achilles had that pesky heel.

3

On-Line Identity Theft

Editor's Introduction

Identity theft affects approximately nine million people annually. Not simply an on-line phenomenon, this particular form of crime occurs whenever someone uses another person's private information, such as their name, credit-card number, or Social Security number, for his or her own gain. While identity theft has been going on for years, the Internet has given thieves new tools for taking advantage of unsuspecting victims. Using on-line techniques such as spam and phishing, they attempt to fool people into sending them personal information. Once the thief has this information, he or she can obtain a credit card or establish a bank account in another person's name, as well as commit a variety of other crimes. Repairing the damage done by these on-line crooks costs a great deal of time and money, and sometimes the damage wrought by an identity theft can take years to undo.

The selections in this chapter concentrate on on-line identity theft and explain how people can protect themselves from cyberthieves. In her article "Online Identity Theft," Brigitte Acoca writes that protecting people's identity on-line "is vital for the future of the Internet economy." Identity theft is said to be the fastest-growing crime in the 21st century, and Acoca writes that education and international cooperation between government agencies are crucial to preventing its spread.

In the next article, "Questions About Online Identity," Reid Goldsborough examines the ways in which people mask their identities on-line. While using handles and false usernames might protect children from predators, the anonymity afforded Internet users can also prove dangerous. "There is no truth-testing online," noted psychologist Joyce Brothers tells Goldsborough, and indeed, even photos can't always be believed. In recent years, doctored images have created problems for everyone from on-line daters to law-enforcement agents.

In "Guard Yourself Against Identity Theft on Social Networks," Pamela Yip considers how sites such as Facebook and MySpace might help facilitate identity theft. Yip posits that since people freely express themselves on these sites, they inadvertently post information that could help thieves steal their identities. For example, a user might mention their mother's maiden name or even the name of their favorite pet. Since the Web sites of many financial institutions ask for this information to ensure that a person trying to log in is who they say they are, such information could be misused. Yip offers tips on how to prevent such outcomes from happening.

The fifth article, "Swiped, Stolen and Sold," is a *New York Times* interview with computer forensics expert Gary Warner. Warner discusses a massive identity-fraud case whereby more than 40 million credit- and debit-card numbers were stolen from major retail stores. He explains the tactics used by the thieves and considers the future of cybercrime detection.

Cryptologist Stefan Brands developed an encryption system called U-Prove that he hopes will give consumers almost perfect protection from identity theft. Alexander Gelfand's article "Startup Plans to Solve Online Identity Theft, But Does Anyone Care?," discusses Brands's startup company, Credentica, and his innovative system.

Online Identity Theft[*]

By Brigitte Acoca
The OECD Observer, July 2008

Would you shop in a store if you knew the credit card machine at the till was likely to send your bank details to an organized gang somewhere abroad?

Such incidents happen every day in the physical world. In fact, credit card fraud from all kinds of real world transactions is a major global crime, and whole government websites are dedicated to fighting it. But it does not stop people from going out to shop with their credit cards. In general, the public trusts that shopping in a physical store is safe, and it generally is. The Internet is quite a safe place to do business too, and, as long as precautions are taken, keying in credit card details on an encrypted webpage is probably safer than, say, calling personal numbers out over the phone to some unknown sales clerk.

But it is a relatively new marketplace, and trust takes time to build up, particularly when transactions take place across borders and recourse in the event of fraud is unclear. This makes online ID theft particularly brutal on its victims, and makes the public that bit more sceptical. Building online confidence is a key challenge not just for the future growth of the Internet economy, but for helping in the fight against all types of cyber fraud, including ID theft.

In the US, nearly a third of adults report that security fears compelled them to shop online less, or not at all, during the 2005–2006 holiday season, according to a survey by the Identity Theft Task Force. In the EU there is a similar pattern of distrust, with three-quarters of people surveyed in an EU report saying that fear of ID theft stopped them purchasing goods or services online. Most of those that did shop online bought goods or services from within the relative safety and comfort of their own countries.

In recent years, a patchwork of public and private sector bodies, and the media, have alerted the public about the threat, at both domestic and international levels.

However, ID theft has been the subject of different legal characterisations in OECD countries, leading to different enforcement schemes. While the US and Canada consider it as a serious crime, EU member states classify it as fraud.

For the OECD, ID theft "occurs when a party acquires, transfers, possesses, or uses personal information of a natural or legal person in an unauthorised manner, with the intent to commit, or in connection with, fraud or other crimes."

A problem for building confidence is that the thieves' techniques keep evolving. Victims' personal information can be mainly obtained through malicious software ('malware') installed on a computer or by "phishing" e-mails and fake websites imitating well-known institutions. Phishing messages increasingly contain malware and are vehicled through spam. All are designed to fool people into disclosing their personal information.

Phishing itself is becoming more sophisticated and difficult to detect, and comes in many forms with somewhat foreboding names. There is "pharming" whereby users are redirected from an authentic to a fraudulent website that replicates the original in appearance. "Spearphishing" is another form, where the sender impersonates a company's employee/employer to steal their colleagues' passwords/usernames. Then there is "vishing," when a spoofed e-mail invites recipients to call a telephone number, where in turn an automated attendant asks users to enter personal information as a security precaution. Clever users that feel they will not be duped by any of these tricks could still be caught out by "SMiShing," where a short text message sent out onto their mobile phone confirms their signing up for a company's services, indicating that they will be charged a fee unless they cancel their order at the company's website. Such website is in fact compromised and used to steal personal information.

Like burglaries, most people believe cyber theft only happens to others. Yet ID theft has been qualified by many as the "fastest growing crime of the 21st century". However, its true scale is difficult to measure. Available statistics are inconsistent from one country or authority to another, complicating cross-border comparisons; most data rely on consumer complaints, but many victims do not report their case to the authorities.

Some security vendors even say that ID theft has declined in recent years. But most believe it has increased. According to the US Federal Trade Commission, in 2006, for the sixth year in a row, ID theft topped the list of consumer complaints, accounting for 246,035 of more than 674,354 fraud complaints filed with the agency.

ID theft has resulted in substantial economic losses for stakeholders, including individual victims, financial institutions, and even whole economies. In the UK, the Home Office estimates that ID fraud costs £1.7 billion (US$330 billion) to the UK economy, nearly 50% up on 2002. According to APACS, the UK payments association, online banking fraud doubled in the first half of 2006 compared with a year earlier.

What can be done to prevent online identity theft? One solution is education. Various member countries have taken initiatives, often in the form of websites, to alert consumers and users about ID theft risks. There are also videos, leaflets and general information kits. The aim is equally to educate businesses about the problem. In Canada, for example, the Consumer Measures Committee has developed an ID theft information kit informing companies on how to reduce the risk of compromising consumers' information, and what to do when a thief strikes.

Another step is to take actions to enhance cross-border enforcement cooperation. The development of a globally accepted concept would help implement dissuasive sanctions. One idea is to impose an obligation on companies to disclose security breaches affecting customers' sensitive personal information. The idea behind it is that if people do not know they are at risk, they are unable to protect themselves against ID theft. Such obligation of disclosure, which has, for example, been established under various US state laws, is under consideration in Australia in the context of the review of the country's privacy laws, but does not yet exist in the EU.

ID management, and more specifically, electronic authentication tools—in short, technology—may also evolve as helpful means to combat online ID theft. In Korea, in 2006, an improved online identity system was introduced. The 13-digit citizen registration number, which contained people's personal information and was used as an online ID verification tool, was replaced by a new "i-PIN" (Internet-only Personal Identification Number) with no personal data, which could be replaced if copied or misused, and which could not be used to trace other website registration information. Such techniques should reduce online ID theft as they do not contain the kind of sensitive information thieves look for.

As ever when it comes to building trust, multi-stakeholder co-operation is a vital part of the answer. In 2007, the UN Office on Drugs and Crime (UNODC) developed a set of recommendations on ID-related crimes (UN, 2007), calling on authorities, the private sector and civil society to join efforts to fight ID theft. The 2008 OECD Ministerial Conference on the Future of the Internet Economy is an opportunity to step up that co-operation and make real progress.

REFERENCES

• European Commission (2006), *Special Eurobarometer: Consumer Protection in the Internal Market*, September 2006, Brussels, at: http://ec.europa_eu/public_opinion/archives/ebs/ebs252_en.pdf

• Federal Trade Commission (2007), *Consumer Fraud and Identity Theft Complaint Data*, at: www.consumer.gov/sentinel/pubs/Top1OFraud 2006.pdf

• Identity Theft Task Force (2007), *Combating Identity Theft: A Strategic Plan*, 23 April 2007, at: www.idtheft.gov

• OECD (2008), *Scoping Paper on Online Identity Theft*, at: www.oecd.org/sti/consumer-policy

• United Nations (2007), "Results of the second meeting of the Intergovernmental Expert Group To Prepare a Study on Fraud and the Criminal Misuse and Falsification of Identity", Report of the Secretary-General, 2 April 2007, E/CN.15/2007/8.

Questions About Online Identity[*]

By Reid Goldsborough
Tech Directions, December 12, 2007

Who am I? Is this real? What does it all mean?

These aren't just questions that a philosophy professor might use to challenge a class of college students. They're also practical considerations everyone faces in the online world. Should you use your real identity in your online discussion groups, blogs, or instant messages? Or should you manufacture a false ID?

SOME USE "HANDLES"

In one Web discussion site I frequent, one of the posters made the comment, "We use handles online." Yes, many people use these chosen nicknames. But not everybody does.

On one recent, random day I analyzed the names used by the 108 people who had logged onto a randomly chosen Web discussion site. Most people used a handle that didn't appear to have any meaning or was some hidden combination of their first and last names with perhaps some extra letters or numbers. The next largest group chose a meaningful handle such as captaincoffee, Dads Stuff, Eagle-eye, homevideo, labmom, lostDutchman, Oldman, superbeast1098, TreasureGirl, and WildJon. Then came those who used what appeared to be their real first names. The smallest group, just three of the 108 people, all of whom were experts or well-known in their field, used their full names.

There are benefits and drawbacks to each approach. Depending on the group, it may be difficult to be taken seriously if you use a handle such as funkypunk. On the other hand, choosing a handle that broadcasts something about your interests, aspirations, or fantasies is a shortcut way for others to peg you.

Sometimes using a handle or assumed name is self-protection by preserving your privacy. One example is participating in a discussion group about a sensitive matter such as spousal abuse or an infectious disease. Another example is wanting to speak freely about politics, religion, or similar topics without worrying about possible repercussions at work.

But cloaking your identity can take on a sinister hue if you create more than one ID to verbally attack others; it can appear psychopathological if you use the false identities to talk with or defend yourself. Such deceptive online identities are derogatively known as "sockpuppets."

Kids have fun making up identities online, indicating that their hometowns are on the planet Jupiter and using pictures of their dogs to illustrate their likenesses. Parents want their kids to protect their identities online to decrease the possibility of predators, who may try to gain the trust of a vulnerable, gullible child with the intent of meeting that child in person.

ONLINE FICTIONALIZATION

The online dating scene brings its own twist to online identity issues. As pop psychologist Joyce Brothers once told me in a telephone interview, "There is no truth-testing online. No one verifies that you are who you say you are." As Peter Steiner wrote in his famous July 5, 1993, New Yorker cartoon, which portrayed a dog typing at a computer, "On the Internet, nobody knows you're a dog."

Those who pretend they're more than they are, in words or in pictures, typically get their just deserts when an online relationship graduates into the real world.

Digital technology makes it easier than ever to fictionalize pictures. Since the introduction of Photoshop in 1990, it and other image-editing programs have let people correct, enhance, or completely change photos with their computers. Perfect white teeth, sparkling eyes, and a face free of wrinkles, freckles, pores, moles, pimples, or other blemishes are just a few mouse clicks away.

The latest digital cameras come with built-in features that can do some of this work automatically. Some Hewlett-Packard cameras include a feature that makes you look thinner without dieting, while some Olympus cameras can give you a Caribbean tan without stepping aboard an airplane.

Pictures that lie have more serious implications than online dating fudging. The Image Science Group at Dartmouth College recently released tools that help the law enforcement community detect photo fraud, and work is underway to do the same with video fraud.

The ultimate in new reality is virtual reality, an old concept that for years has promised a totally immersive experience incorporating all of the senses. Wearing "data outfits," we'll not only see and hear the sights and sounds of the simulated environment, but feel, smell, and taste it as well.

In the meantime, being firmly grounded in reality means appreciating the differences between the online world and the real world. If used wisely, the Internet and computer technology can, in general, enhance your quality of life. If used unwisely, you're just a nerd at your computer on Saturday night.

Guard Yourself Against Identity Theft on Social Networks[*]

By Pamela Yip
The Dallas Morning News, December 8, 2008

The next source of identity theft may be social networking Web sites.

"There's a growing problem, and the risks are increasing," said Scott Mitic, chief executive of TrustedID, which has identity-theft protection products for consumers and businesses.

Officials of the Federal Trade Commission, which enforces identity theft laws, said they know of no ID theft cases that have arisen from social networking sites, but you can't be too careful.

Thieves are constantly searching for new ways to get you to divulge any sliver of personal information so they can tap into your wallet.

And social networking sites such as MySpace and Facebook are becoming a "growing pool of valuable information that at some point thieves may consider more valuable than a credit report," Mr. Mitic said.

For example, most of us use facts associated with our lives as user words or passwords, and thieves are learning they can mine these facts from social networking sites.

"I know most Americans who, if they have pets, that's usually their password," Mr. Mitic said. "The information that may seem innocuous to share may have real value to individuals with criminal minds."

Social networking sites enable people to freely express themselves in a way that may cause them to unwittingly drop morsels of information that criminals can extract to steal their identity.

Here's how it might work:

Your profile says that you live in Texas, you were born in Dallas, your beloved pet's name is Max and that you like to spend time with your parents, Dick and Jane.

It also says that today you're venting your anger at your bank—Bank XYZ— because it's been slow to resolve a problem with your account.

Now criminals know the name of your bank, the name of your pet and your mother's name. They will seek to learn your mother's maiden name, which is often used as a security question on bank Web sites.

Here are some tips to protect yourself online. You've heard them before, but they're particularly important for social networking sites because the information you post can be accessed by others:

- Never post sensitive personal data, such as your Social Security number, driver's license number and bank account numbers.

  That includes your hometown, mother's maiden name, your date of birth, your high school, the hospital or city in which you were born and your favorite color.

  "There are all of these secret-password answer questions," Mr. Mitic said.

- Avoid telling everyone your physical location and what you're doing at the very moment, especially if you're away from home. That's an invitation for someone to burglarize your home.

- Manage privacy controls on social networks. Set your profile to "Private" to prevent uninvited people from viewing your personal information.

- Don't make your password easy to guess.

- Only allow people you know to view your personal profile. Be careful about allowing strangers to view your profile because people aren't always who they say they are.

Officials of social networking site Facebook said they give users tools to protect themselves.

"Facebook users' profiles are by default accessible only to confirmed friends and others in a given network, and we've put in place additional protections for more sensitive information like phone number, e-mail, and home address," said spokesman Simon Axten. "Users can control access to information as they see fit using the extensive and particular settings we offer."

Users of MySpace also can control how visitors and other MySpace members communicate with them by controlling their account settings.

It reminds users that their personal profile and MySpace forums are public spaces and advises users to not post sensitive personal information.

Many of you will see this advice and say it's unrealistic because I'm practically muzzling you. But you have to decide how much information you want to share.

"How safe do you want to be?" Mr. Mitic said. "How risky a lifestyle do you want to live? We live in a world where it can be dangerous to publicly expose personal information about yourself. If you want to live a safer life, you need to be more protective of your information."

Bottom line: Have fun but be safe.

Swiped, Stolen and Sold[*]

The New York Times, August 6, 2008

The Justice Department says it has broken open the largest identity fraud case so far in the United States, indicting 11 people around the world in the theft of more than 40 million credit and debit card numbers from computer networks at TJ Maxx stores and other big retailers. The Times asked Gary Warner, the director of research in computer forensics at the University of Alabama at Birmingham who writes a blog about cyber crime, to discuss the significance of the announcement.

Q. How are the identity fraud indictments announced this week different from previous cases?

A. This is the biggest case filed so far in terms of financial losses in cyber crimes. Some very significant wholesalers have been identified—the guys in China probably represented Asia in this operation. By breaking up the brokers, there will be some reorganization period while things get shifted around. The Justice Department also treated this as an intelligence operation. They didn't just arrest one guy quickly. They built a case around a larger network.

The question is how much has law enforcement really got, and I'm hoping we'll see a whole new round of arrests. They say they have the hacker, Albert Gonzalez—Segvec—of Miami. What did he do with the credentials he allegedly stole? If he gave them all to the Ukrainian, Maksym Yastremskiy, who was arrested in a Turkish night club, what did he do with the numbers? There are 40 million credit cards hanging out there, so we're all still at risk. Even if you cut up your credit card and get a new one, what has happened to the information compiled on your old one?

Q. It turns out that the main suspect in the case filed in Boston, Albert Gonzalez, was a government informant, and some reports say he may have tipped off members of his alleged ring with information he got from law enforcement. What does that say about this case?

A. When dealing with confidential informants, it's often a case of knowing what to ask them. You might have someone who comes to your attention because he is very knowledgeable about wireless hacking. Maybe it's someone who worked a local computer store. You may talk with them once a week, or only once a month, and you will have decided to limit your scope of questions to wireless hacking. So you ask about what wi-fi antennas are being used, and what the ranges are, and what the most common places to "ride wi-fi" in the area are. And because of the scope you chose for this relationship, it never comes up that this guy is ALSO an expert on credit card trading rings, and good friends with three of the top suspects in a case being worked in another field office.

Unfortunately, you can't really give them a list of all open cases and say "read these and let me know if you know any of the folks in there."

In this particular case we are also challenged by geographic and linguistic barriers. It's quite possible that a large part of the credit card trading wasn't happening in English, and it's quite possible that the best places to do this trading are only open by invitation to people who have met in person in the past. Even among criminals there is a "ring of trust," where only people who have been validated by a personal relationship are allowed "inside."

Q. TJX, the parent company of TJ Maxx, has already paid Visa and other credit card companies many tens of millions of dollars to cover the costs of the fraud. At what point does the consumer start paying the bill?

A. The consumer is already paying the bill. Banks and credit card merchants will say that it hasn't hurt the consumer, because it's included in "the price of doing business," but "the price of doing business" affects profit margins, which in turn affect stockholder value, which in turn affects pricing of goods. If TJX paid a penalty, they made up that somewhere else. Probably on their price tags.

Q. It seems amazing that the news of massive identity-theft cases doesn't make newspapers' most-emailed lists. Is it because the consumer is still protected in some way?

A. The problem is that there is not an empathy-evoking poster child for cyber crime. In one portion of the charges filed in an earlier part of the case, hackers supposedly sat in a car, broke into the point-of-sale terminals at the Dave & Buster's chain, installed "sniffer" software, and from that point forward, every credit card swiped at that terminal sent all of its data to the hackers. No customers did anything wrong, but neither have we been able to show the sad story of people who lost their life savings due to recharging their video game cards at D&B's. Several journalists contacted me after that case, and they all wanted to know the same thing: "Can you put us in touch with someone who had a significant financial loss due to that case?" No. We have millions of anonymous users who may have unauthorized charges on their credit cards. Can we prove what sloppy transaction caused that loss? In the majority of cases, no.

Their data is harvested, bulked together with other data, and sold by criminal wholesalers, who may later dip into their limitless supply of credit card info, and choose to make a card belonging to that victim. We have "rolled up" data, like the Consumer Sentinel reports from the F.T.C. telling us that 800,000 people had reported actual loss of $1.2 billion in fraud and identity theft in 2007, but it's hard to get the actual people to make the compelling stories.

On the other hand, we could try to make the brands look irresponsible and careless, as if they are treating your data with whimsical disregard. The truth is though that ALMOST EVERYONE is vulnerable to this type of attack. There was some outcry that they had violated PCI standards (the rules for credit card merchants to follow), but the standards are nebulous and open to great ranges of interpretation. Several very large credit card leaks have come from companies who had passed audits showing themselves to be "PCI Compliant."

Q. What are the new frontiers in cyber crime? What areas—either geographical or technological—are the criminals pursuing that they hadn't invaded, say, a year ago?

A. As we move to Web 2.0, and more and more Web pages require users to trust their Web server in order for the content to load properly, we are seeing a huge increase in "drive-by infections." If someone visits a Web site, BOOM, they are infected. The same basic security that would prevent most of that from happening, also makes your sexy high-tech Web page look like crap, because my "secure" browser won't allow any of your widgets to run. We are looking at a case right now where more than THREE MILLION Web pages are infected with such drive-by infection code. That's just one case.

Geographically, we're still having basic justice problems in nations with depressed economies. There are still countries where the rule of law is "he who has U.S. dollars rules." Cyber thieves have many U.S. dollars, and they are beyond the law in many of these nations. At some point it goes to being a problem not for the Justice Department but for the State and Commerce departments to solve.

Q. Is there anything that puzzles you about the case this week?

A. I can't figure out the Chinese angle. Two Chinese nationals were identified, but not arrested. What we do know is that the Chinese government—either through complacency or conspiracy—has allowed bulletproof hosting. By "bulletproof hosting," I mean that if I'm hosting a credit card trading forum, I have to guarantee that I have a reliable server that will never be taken down, and that requires some understanding with local law enforcement. Can I do this in the United States? No. We know that Russians buy these bulletproof hosting sites from China. I don't know if the Ukrainian and Estonian suspects are linked to China. We do know that China is a haven for many cyber criminals who run bulletproof servers, and we do know that Eastern Europeans and Russians are frequently customers of those services. Perhaps that's how they met, but at this point it's just speculation.

Startup Plans to Solve Online Identity Theft, But Does Anyone Care?*

By Alexander Gelfand
Wired, February 8, 2008

Imagine you could prove you were 21 without revealing your date of birth—or anything else about you, for that matter. Or qualify for a loan without disclosing your net worth. Or enjoy the benefits of e-commerce, e-health and e-government without a moment's fear that you are open to identity theft.

Sound impossible? It is. But it won't be if cryptographer and entrepreneur Stefan Brands has his way.

Brands runs Credentica, a Montreal-based startup that is rolling out an encryption-and-authentication system called U-Prove that allows users to disclose the absolute minimum to complete digital transactions—and to do so in a way that ensures the information they need to reveal has no shelf life whatsoever.

"By protecting privacy, you can actually enhance security," Brands says. "My goal is to get the best of both worlds."

Maintaining digital privacy and security has never been more important. As more and more people trust their personal information to electronic databases, security and privacy are plummeting. More than 79 million personal electronic records containing data like credit card and Social Security numbers were compromised in the United States last year—almost four times the number reported in 2006, according to the San Diego-based Identity Theft Resource Center. And more than 162 million such records were compromised globally, more than three times 2006 levels, according to Attrition.org.

Here's the problem: Every time you use a credit card, somebody you didn't actually give it to could be squirreling the numbers away.

"If you walk through a shopping center, you don't have your personal information pinned to your shirt in a way that anyone you deal with can just walk up and read it," says Kim Cameron, Microsoft's chief architect of identity and author of the Identity Weblog. "You control the information you release."

Over time, the problem compounds: Buy something here, provide an address there, use your driver's license number somewhere else. "In the digital world, information leaks, and super-profiles can be assembled, just through continued use of the internet," Cameron says.

U-Prove promises security by revealing as little as possible and rendering what is disclosed useless for anything but the transaction at hand.

The technique employs secure multi-party computation, a branch of cryptography that can calculate meaningful answers about secret information by knowing only some nonrevealing clues about that secret. The underlying theory was demonstrated in 1982 by Andrew Yao in the so-called Millionaire's Problem: Alice and Bob want to find out who has more money without disclosing the amount of their fortunes to each other, or even to a mutually trusted third party. By applying special functions to their information that disguised it, Yao proved that each could know who was richer without either revealing their true holdings.

U-Prove employs an ID token, a special kind of digital certificate that allows for minimal selective disclosure. The tokens can store all kinds of information, but users can disclose only the minimum amount of data required in any given transaction. They leave no unwanted data trails and permit both anonymity and pseudonymity.

The tokens are also loaded with cryptographic protections that make them resistant to phishing, forgery and all manner of online security woes. They cannot be traced back to their issuers. Separate tokens used by the same person cannot be linked together.

As a result, neither the people who create the tokens nor those who accept them can track and correlate their use. And users need never reveal more than they would like.

Credentica VP of engineering Greg Thompson says that's not the case with certificates generated by public key infrastructure, the cryptographic system that has long been the most common means of authenticating identities and encrypting messages online.

In conventional public key cryptography, Thompson says, "the math itself gives you linking and tracing, whether you want it or not."

The U-Prove approach has been tried before, without commercial success. Most companies tried to sell privacy software to consumers, which was the wrong approach.

So Brands is flipping it around by developing a software developers kit that would appeal to businesses and government agencies that want to prevent costly and damaging data breaches on behalf of their customers.

In addition, Brands hopes that by providing a somewhat stripped-down version of his technology under a noncommercial license he can encourage developers to explore its potential applications—just like RSA Data Security did in the 1980s when it offered free, noncommercial use of its public-key cryptosystem and went on to dominate the online security market.

"They were a small company," Brands says. "Now everybody knows who RSA is."

Credentica is in licensing talks with several large original equipment manufacturers, and Brands hopes to announce one or more deals shortly.

It can still be a tough sell. Most technical personnel continue to think of attacks from outsiders—not abuse or collusion by insiders—as the primary threat to personal data. And for nontechnical personnel, the theory underlying ID tokens can be daunting. Both Brands and Thompson tend to refer to the math behind U-Prove as "magic" rather than going too deep into the details.

In the meantime, U-Prove is generating some street cred.

"I think that U-Prove adds a really interesting dimension to the discussion around identity, by allowing people to make claims which are authenticated, but not associated with a person," says Adam Shostack, a former cypherpunk who worked with Brands at Zero Knowledge Systems and now works at Microsoft.

"I remember when I saw my first driver's license scanner at a bar in Boston," Shostack says. "I didn't want the bar capturing everything on my license so they could prove due diligence in not letting minors drink. U-Prove lets me prove my age, without providing anything else about me."

4

Internet Safety for Teens and Children

Editor's Introduction

Relative to prior generations, today's young people are remarkably tech-savvy. Having grown up with cell phones and the Internet, children and teenagers navigate cyberspace with ease. While their comfort with technology is a good thing, many youngsters are quick to post photos and other private information, unwittingly leaving themselves open to cybercriminals.

This chapter focuses on Internet safety as it pertains to children and teenagers. Considering the popularity of cell phones, MySpace, Facebook, Twitter, instant messaging, Skype, Photobucket, and other on-line applications and Web sites, young people have countless opportunities to share personal information. To thwart the efforts of those who would take advantage of such information, parents, educators, and law-enforcement agencies are improving the ways in which they monitor children's Internet usage. The articles herein discuss various types of on-line threats, including those posed by cyberbullies and sexual predators.

In the first article, "Kids Put Online Safety First," Marianne McGee lists a number of Web sites and programs designed to keep children safe while surfing the Web. Such protections are particularly useful during the summer months, she writes, when children have more free time to spend using the Internet.

In their piece "When Teens Turn Cyberbullies," Paris and Robert Strom describe the phenomenon of cyberbullying, or online harassment. Unlike conventional bullies, cyberbullies are relatively anonymous, free from the oversight of teachers and parents. As a result, they tend to be less inhibited and more aggressive, using e-mail, chat rooms, instant messages, text messages, and cell phones to target their prey. The authors highlight the differences between traditional bullying and cyberbullying and explore ways to curtail the problem.

In the third article, "Patrolling Web 2.0," Robert Losinski describes on-line safety measures enacted by the Denver Public School district. He gives advice on protecting students on social-networking sites and discusses the risks of using such Web sites as Facebook and MySpace.

In "Sex Predator," the fourth selection, Asra Q. Nomani tells the story of Dianna Strawder, a woman whose fiancee was featured on the popular television show *Dateline: To Catch a Predator*. Strawder's fiancee allegedly tried to solicit sex from an underage girl, who was actually a decoy working for the show. *To Catch a Predator* aims to apprehend adults trying to set up sexual liaisons with underage children and teens. The targets meet decoys in chatrooms or on social-networking sites and are lured into houses where they are confronted and subsequently arrested. The article examines the painful aftermath of Strawder's fiancee's arrest and details how the incident affected the family.

The next piece, "Survey Finds Teens Solicit Students More than Adult Predators," offers a bit of a reality check to those overly worried about adults targeting children, revealing that, by and large, it is not adults but fellow students and teens who are sending inappropriate e-mails to one another.

Megan Meier was, in many ways, a typical teenager. Although friendly and cheerful, she had low self-esteem and was depressed as a child. Lori Drew, the mother of a former friend, created a fake MySpace profile, disguising herself as a slightly older boy named Josh Evans. Drew reportedly initiated the ploy as a way of finding out what Megan was saying about her own daughter. The encounter eventually led to Megan's suicide. While this case was discussed briefly in the first chapter, in "Lori Drew Is a Meanie," Emily Bazelon explores it further, arguing that the verdict raises concerns about on-line freedom of speech.

Boasting more than 250 million members, many of them teenagers, MySpace is among the world's most popular social-networking Web sites. In "Decoding MySpace," Michelle Andrews looks at safety issues associated with the site. In light of highly publicized stories of predators luring minors into sexual situations, Andrews explains how teenagers use MySpace and offers parents tips for keeping their children out of harm's way. Similarly, in her article "Online Photos Put Hazing in the Spotlight Again," Stacy Teicher discusses how hazing—common among collegiate fraternities and sports teams—has evolved in the digital age. Teicher reports that many college athletes post photos of hazing rituals that include drinking and sexual activity.

Kids Put Online Safety First[*]

By Marianne Kolbasuk McGee
InformationWeek, July 4, 2005

School's out and kids are looking for something to do. Millions—more than 77 million, according to the U.S. Department of Justice—will jump on the Net during the summer months, exposing themselves to potential danger, including online predators, other cybercriminals, and harassment from fellow kids.

But grassroots efforts are under way to make the online world safer for young people, including groups of kids working to keep each other safe online. These youngsters are educating each other on protecting themselves and their privacy on the Internet. Technology vendors, including Microsoft, and other companies such as Walt Disney Co. are using kids' input to improve the safety of their products and services. Their awareness level is rising to the point that they're also getting directly involved in efforts to keep kids safe.

WiredKids—through its TeenAngels program for kids ages 13 to 18 launched in 1999 and its newer offshoot program, TweenAngels, for preteens—educates young people, parents, and teachers about safe and responsible use of the Internet, interactive game consoles such as Microsoft Xbox, and other technologies such as cell phones. There are 19 TeenAngels chapters in the United States—in California, Maryland, New Jersey, New York, Wisconsin, and soon Alaska—and several in the United Kingdom.

Input from TeenAngels has encouraged some vendors to tweak features of their products and services. For instance, meetings between Microsoft product planners in the United Kingdom and a group of British TeenAngels helped inspire new safety features in MSN Space Groups products and services, which allow users to build their own Weblogs, says Pam Portin, Microsoft's director of MSN policy.

Work between Microsoft and other teen groups also helped in the development of safety features in Microsoft Xbox Live, which lets kids play interactive video games with others via the Internet. Reporting features help Microsoft monitor or investigate complaints about cyberbullying or other inappropriate or harassing behaviors among kids using Xbox Live, Portin says.

Further enhancements, bolstered by input from kids, will show up in improved parental controls in the next version of Xbox, called Xbox 360, scheduled to debut this holiday season, Portin says.

For Microsoft, getting input from kids is a no-brainer. "The ability for our products and services to be used safely is important to us," Portin says.

Adolescents from organizations such as TeenAngels give presentations to vendors or participate in focus groups with a great deal of knowledge and expertise that can influence how technology products and services will be built with an eye to online safety. In fact, they're doing some of the building themselves. Because so many kids are more Internet-literate than their parents, one Wisconsin TeenAngel conceived of and designed an online chat-lingo translator to help parents decipher the E-mail and instant-messaging shorthand and codes young people use to communicate with one another.

Kids who participate in TeenAngels and TweenAngels are trained by law-enforcement agencies, including the FBI, and Internet privacy experts, such as Parry Aftab, who founded the not-for-profit WiredKids to help educate children on safe use of the Web. For instance, in May, during a trip to the Washington, D.C., area to attend an annual WiredKids summit, a group of TeenAngels attended training at an FBI cybercrime facility in Maryland. There they were able to see technology used by the agency to track possible pedophiles pretending to be kids online.

Once fully trained, TeenAngels go back into their communities to educate at least 500 other kids, including younger schoolmates, about safe use of the Internet. The education includes teaching about the four P's: privacy, predators, pornography, and piracy. Kids are taught how to protect passwords; not to share personal information online; and how to avoid spyware, malicious code, unscrupulous Web sites, con artists, sexual predators, and other cybercriminals. Angels also learn how to handle cyberbullying, a form of harassment using technology, and how to avoid becoming a cyberbully.

"Kids get great experience, and they help to mentor other kids," says Aftab, a privacy lawyer and *InformationWeek* columnist.

Brittany Bacon, now a 21-year-old college senior, was one of the five founding members of TeenAngels when Aftab launched the first chapter in 1999 at an all-girls Catholic high school in Bergen County, N.J. Since then, Bacon has helped create several TeenAngel chapters, including two in the United Kingdom. During a recent internship in the British Parliament, Bacon, along with Aftab and law enforcement from the United States and Europe's Interpol, met with members of Parliament to brief them on Internet safety issues.

"We're trying to help kids help other kids," Bacon says. Kids "can be part of the problem, but they can also be part of the solution," she says about keeping young people safe and out of trouble on the Web.

Before becoming a TeenAngel, Bacon admits she, like many of her friends, illegally downloaded music using services such as Kazaa. But after learning about piracy through her TeenAngel training, she stopped and has gotten lots of other kids to stop, too. "It's not right and it's unfair to illegally download music and movies," she says. Besides helping kids be ethical in their online behavior, TeenAngels can prevent piracy lawsuits against parents, she adds. In fact, all of her TeenAngels education in cyberlaw has Bacon interested in going to law school.

Members of TeenAngels and TweenAngels aren't the only kids that Microsoft works with. In June, the company held a "pilot" kids' safety summit, the first in what the software maker expects to be an annual event to bring kids together to educate them on Internet safety, privacy, piracy, cyberbullying and more, Portin says. The company invited children from San Diego County to participate in the daylong event designed to teach the youngsters about being "cybersmart." The event was co-sponsored by I-Safe, another children's online safety-awareness organization aimed at educating parents, teachers, and kids.

I-Safe provides educational programs for schools, in which young people are trained by law enforcement, guidance counselors, and others. I-Safe-trained high-school students can receive school credit for mentoring younger kids or creating activities to pass the word on about Internet safety. The group provides training materials free to the schools, president Teri Schroeder says. Microsoft is developing interactive, Web-based I-Safe curriculum to educate teachers, Schroeder says.

Working with groups to help teach kids about online safety is important, Microsoft's Portin says. "There's a strong commitment from Microsoft. We take our responsibility to raise awareness very seriously," she says. Microsoft is looking to partner with organizations such as TeenAngels and I-Safe that have this core competency of helping to educate kids on safe Internet use, she says.

Meanwhile, WiredKids is in the early stages of forming a partnership with technology-industry organization the Cellular Telecommunications and Internet Association. Together, they hope to create outreach programs that could include videos and brochures to educate parents, teachers, and children about mobile-phone safety. That includes making parents aware that kids can access the Internet— including mature Web sites—from some cell phones, says Carolyn Brandon, the association's VP of policy.

Besides tech vendors, other businesses, including entertainment companies, are relying on kids to help improve the Web safety of their products and services.

Disney Online works with kids to develop new features and services for its interactive online products, including ToonTown Online, an Internet-based playground, and the upcoming PlayHouse Disney Preschool Time Online, a learning-based broadband service for preschool-age children slated to launch in the fall. Disney Online product developers regularly get feedback from young people via focus groups, input from kids groups like TeenAngels, and Disney Online's own developers' children and their friends.

Behind the ToonTown online platform, Disney has "very sophisticated proprietary" filtering software that helps keep kids in line and safe, says Ken Goldstein, executive VP at Disney Online. For instance, swear words are automatically deleted from online chatter. Identifying information that kids attempt to exchange with one another, such as phone numbers, is also blocked to prevent the information from falling into the wrong hands, Goldstein says.

"We can see from a mile away aggressive behavior," he says. And Disney doesn't tolerate such behavior. On occasion, it has revoked the accounts of kids who have behaved aggressively or inappropriately, Goldstein says.

A group of TeenAngels has tested and used ToonTown and made recommendations to Disney Online—which the company acted on—to remove the ability for kids younger than 13 to post their photos on the site, TeenAngel Bacon says.

With more than 10,000 people logging on to ToonTown every day, Disney Online developers and software engineers are more than eager to listen to the suggestions of kids, whether it's for fun or safety. "The Internet has redefined the playground," Goldstein says, and parents and kids all want a safe and fun place to play.

When Teens Turn Cyberbullies*

By Paris S. Strom and Robert D. Strom
The Education Digest, December 2005

Cyber harassment involves using an electronic medium to threaten or harm others. E-mail, chat rooms, cell phones, instant messaging, pagers, text messaging, and online voting booths are tools used to inflict humiliation, fear, and a sense of helplessness. This type of intimidation differs from traditional bullying in several important ways.

Unlike the incidents that most adults recall from their youth, where the threatening party is physically bigger and more powerful than the victim, cyberbullies can be physically weaker than the persons they attempt to frighten. Cyberbullies typically hide behind the mask of anonymity that the Internet provides by using fictitious screen names.

Because abusers may lack face-to-face contact with the individuals being persecuted, they may not know the level of duress that is produced by their misconduct. Therefore, they are unlikely to experience feelings of regret, sympathy, or compassion toward the victim.

MORE DAMAGING

Harmful messages intended to undermine the reputation of a victim can be far more damaging than face-to-face altercations. Instead of remaining a private matter or event known by only a small group, text or photographs can be communicated to a large audience in a short time.

Whereas bullies at school usually can be identified easily by mistreated individuals, cyberbullies typically are difficult to trace. Consequently, they can avoid responsibility for their misconduct, thereby reducing the fear of getting caught and being punished.

Cyberspace represents new territory for peer mistreatment, often leaving school administrators with doubts about the boundaries of their jurisdiction. School leaders may be unable to respond when unknown parties have sent hate messages from a location outside the school, such as from a home-based computer or mobile phone.

Some students are reluctant to tell adults about the anxiety they endure at the hands of cyber enemies, fearing that parents may overreact by taking away their computer, Internet access, or cell phone. Many teenagers are unwilling to risk having their parents choose such extreme forms of protection because, without technology tools, they would feel socially isolated and less able to stay in immediate contact with their friends.

A misconception about cyber abuse is that nothing can be done about it. In reality, cyber harassment is a crime that resembles other forms of unlawful behavior and is subject to prosecution.

The University of Dayton School of Law offers numerous resources for the purpose of understanding the legal issues which are related to cyberbullying. The website www.cybercrimes.net describes cyber stalking and cyber intimidation, identifies agencies which are available to be contacted in order to find help in the matter of dealing with cyber mistreatment, offers guidelines which can be used for reporting abuse, and presents articles explaining legal processes and penalties related to a wide range of cyber crimes.

Until recently, the victims of bullying considered their homes a place of safety, a sanctuary which they could take from abusive peers. This is no longer the case in an era of instant, electronic communications.

Most students who are at the secondary school level go online soon after they return home from school. When they arrive there, some discover that they are the target of threats, rumors, and lies without knowing the identity of the persons creating fear and frustration, and most of these students don't know how to stop the damage. The following examples of adolescent cyberbullying in several countries reveal the range and complexity of the issues which are actually involved here.

Shinobu is a high school freshman in Osaka, Japan. When his gym period was over, he got dressed in what he believed was the privacy of the school changing room. However, a classmate who wanted to ridicule him for being overweight secretly used a cell phone to photograph him. Within seconds, the picture of the naked boy was sent wirelessly by instant messaging for many students to see. By the time he finished dressing and went on to his next class, he had already become a laughing stock of the school.

Sixteen-year-old Denise is a high school junior in Los Angeles, California. Denise had an argument with her boyfriend and broke up with him. The rejected young man was angry and decided that he would get even with her for having broken up with him. The devious method that he chose to use was to post Denise's contact numbers, including her e-mail address, her cell phone number, and her street address, on several sex-oriented websites and blogs.

As a result of her former boyfriend's actions, Denise was hounded for months by instant messages, prank callers, and car horns of insensitive people who drove by her house to see whether or not they could catch a glimpse of her. In this particular case, the identity of the cyberbully, her former boyfriend, was detected quickly. However, his apprehension did not eliminate the sustained sense of helplessness and embarrassment which Denise had experienced.

OFTEN JEALOUSY

Jealousy is a common motive for cyber abuse. Fourteen-year-old Amy lives in Montgomery, Alabama. She is enrolled in a home school curriculum and plans to earn a high school diploma by the time she has reached the age of 16 so she can start college early. Darin, a neighbor who attends public school, is Amy's friend. His girlfriend began sending Amy e-mail messages threatening to cut herself if Amy did not stop talking to Darin.

The guilt that someone might do herself bodily harm because of her led Amy to tell Darin about the e-mails. Darin confessed that his girlfriend had cut herself once before. Amy wanted to do the right thing, but she did not know who to contact. She told her mother, and the police were called to investigate the matter.

Donna attends eighth grade at a parochial school in Montreal, Quebec, Canada. She and her mother traveled to Toronto for a week to visit her grandmother, who was recuperating from cancer surgery. When Donna returned to school, a cyberbully circulated a rumor alleging that Donna had contracted SARS (Severe Acute Respiratory Syndrome) during the course of her stay in Toronto. Donna's girlfriends were scared and unwilling to be around her or even to talk over the phone. Without exception, her classmates moved away from Donna whenever she went near them.

Some cases may involve more than one bully and a single victim. Others could involve a gang of bullies that persecute multiple parties. The latter occurs when students respond to online trash polling sites.

These sites, which are growing in number, invite students to identify individuals by unflattering characteristics, such as the most obese person at their school, the boys who are most likely to be gay, and the girls who have slept with the most boys. The predictable consequences for students who have been subjected to this shameful treatment are depression, hopelessness, and withdrawal.

Students are not the only people at school who are bullied. Teachers often are targets too. When students make disrespectful comments to a teacher or challenge the authority of the school to govern their behavior on campus, they usually are sent to the office, where an administrator examines the situation and determines a suitable course of disciplinary action.

ONLY SO FAR

The limitations of this type of practice for use in preventing student harassment of faculty members are illustrated by the experience of Joseph, a high school teacher in Phoenix, Arizona. He offered computer classes to juniors and seniors and consistently received high ratings from students for his instruction. He was known for preparing students to obtain a good-paying job immediately after graduation.

Joseph felt disappointment and shock when told of a website on which he was the focus of messages on "What I hate about my teacher, Mr. . . . " The site contained statements that Joseph recognized as characteristic of a particular student and comments he recalled saying to the student. Joseph related, "I taught this young man how to apply a technological tool for constructive purposes, and he decided to use it against me."

Some sophisticated adolescent cyberbullies target schools or other institutions by releasing worms that can compromise the integrity of computers or make them unavailable. The result is often disruption leading to significant loss of time and money.

The U.S. Department of Justice website, www.cybercrime.gov, lists prosecuted criminals and a summary of computer intrusion cases, including the juvenile or adult status of perpetrators, type of harm done, estimated dollar loss, target group, geography, and punishment.

That list includes one hacker who directed worm-infected computers to launch a distributed denial of service attack against the Microsoft main website, causing a shutdown and making it inaccessible to the public for four hours. The hacker was 14 years old and pleaded guilty in 2004 to intentionally causing damage and attempting to disable protected computers.

What actions should be taken to reduce the scale of cyberbullying? State departments of education have begun to provide training for administrators in middle and high schools to build awareness of available options in confronting such problems.

Other individuals at schools also should assume responsibility for prevention. The district's information technology staff members could be given the task of designing and delivering K–12 curriculum of acquaint students, teachers, and parents with etiquette on the Internet, methods of self-protection, and ways of responding to persecution.

A related initiative would be to help the adult public recognize that adolescents interact with technology differently than older people. Most grown-ups think of computers as practical tools that can be used to locate information and send electronic mail without the expense of postage stamps. In contrast, teenagers consider instant messaging and chat rooms to be an essential aspect of their social lives—a vital connection with peers. Chat is the number one online activity among teenagers.

WHY ADULTS FALL

These generational differences account for why few adults are able to provide wise counsel on dealing with cyberbullies. The solutions most often proposed are simplistic and result in minimal protection.

For example, purchasing and setting online filters would appear to be suitable solutions, because these preventive measures block reception of unwanted messages. However, by altering their screen names, bullies can override these obstructions easily.

Responding to bullies online in an attempt to persuade them to stop the harassment also might seem to be a reasonable counter. Yet, student experience shows that this approach can motivate a bully to apply even more severe methods of intimidation.

Parents and teachers can follow some practical guidelines to minimize the likelihood of cyberbullying:

- Adults should develop close communications with adolescents and encourage them to relate problems such as episodes of digital harassment.
- Students should be told not to share personal information, such as their e-mail password, with anyone except a parent.
- Students, parents, educators, and law enforcement personnel should know where to go for information about online abuses, such as cyber intimidation, con artists, identity thieves, predators, stalkers, criminal hackers, financial fraud, security, and privacy problems.

  The site WiredSafety, http://wiredsafety.org, is an organization that provides assistance in this area. The U.S. Department of Justice, www.cybercrime.gov, offers guidelines on cyber ethics for students, parents, and teachers and identifies government contacts for reporting Internet crimes. Bill Belsey, recipient of the Canadian Prime Minister's Award for Teaching Excellence in Science, Mathematics, and Technology, maintains www.cyberbullying.ca, a website for students, parents, and the public that describes the emotional costs of cyberbullying, forms of mistreatment, and prevention strategies.
- Adults should ensure that students realize that people may not be who they say they are in a chat room. For example, someone could claim to be a 14-year-old female, but in actuality be a 50-year-old male predator seeking to take advantage of a vulnerable adolescent.
- Teenagers should never agree to meet someone they have chatted with online unless their parents go with them and the meeting is in a public place.
- People should avoid sending impulse messages or staying online when they are angry. Wait until self-control and a sense of calm is restored so that the message is more sensibly written and excludes hostility. People typically regret sending a "flame" (angry) message that could motivate someone to become a cyberbully as an act of revenge for it. Keep in mind that messages

written in capital letters are interpreted as shouting by some recipients.

- When adolescents tell teachers or parents about cyber harassment, the cooperating adults should immediately inform the police and the Internet instant messaging or mobile phone service provider.
- Victims never should respond to cyberbullies, but always should keep messages as evidence, including the text and source of information detailing the originating address of the e-mail. Whether or not they are read, messages should not be erased. The police, the Internet service provider, or the telephone company often can use the narratives for tracking purposes.
- Those who are persecuted might notice words used by certain people they know. Most cyberbullies who post anonymous messages are not as anonymous as they may think. If a legitimate threat exists, law enforcement officials can subpoena records of all web users for a particular website. From there, users can be tracked to their individual computers.

The mission of Channel One, a broadcast network viewed daily in some American classrooms, is to keep secondary school students informed of current events and teach them how the media works. Its website presents an interactive quiz that adolescents, parents, and teachers can complete to check their knowledge about coping with bullies in cyberspace.

The quiz includes questions on instant messaging, threatening e-mails, revealing photographs, personal information, screen name selection, cell phone flames, chat room conflicts, blocking options, and group persecution. Immediate feedback is provided for every response, along with an explanation of the correct answers and a final score. The website, www.channelone.com/news/2004/01/30/cyberbullies/index.html, provides complete information on this interactive quiz.

Cyberbullying is of such recent origin that current understanding is limited. Many parents misinterpret adolescents' time on the Internet as learning rather than considering that it might be related to peer abuse.

This preliminary assessment hopes to begin conversations and encourage studies on ways to confront this new form of abuse. Some challenges include the identification of cyberbullies, encouragement for victims to report abuse, access to counseling for those who suffer persecution, curriculum to guide civil behavior online, rehabilitation programs to help dysfunctional youngsters, parent education to improve their monitoring and guidance functions, and the linkage of institutions for cooperation across jurisdictions.

NO SUCH MAGIC

In fiction, Harry Potter possessed magical powers that he relied on to silence his bully, the abominable Dudley Dursely. In real life, however, adolescents, parents, teachers, and principals do not have such magic at their disposal.

Creativity and persistence are powerful resources that can be applied. Effective methods must be developed for protecting students from being bullied and preventing others from becoming tyrants on the cyber stage. Dumbledore, the Headmaster of Hogwarts School, urged the young wizard Harry to remember, "It is our choices, Harry, that show what we truly are, far more than our abilities."

Condensed from The Educational Forum, *70 (Fall 2005), 21–36.*

Patrolling Web 2.0[*]

By Robert Losinski
T.H.E. Journal, March 2007

As recently as 10 years ago, school computers were the purview of office administrators and limited library use. Most districts didn't have a website, and few anticipated a day when students would be toting laptops from class to class.

Today, districts not only provide students with internet access, they expect the students to leverage it to perform educational research and complete assignments. But while school districts have become more technologically sophisticated, most schools remain a step behind students—and external threats to student well-being.

Students today are a generation raised on Google, e-mail, and instant messaging. In 2005, Pew Internet American Life Project (http://www.pewinternet.org) published a report that said more than 87 percent of American kids ages 12 to 17 were using the internet, and we can be sure that number has increased in the interim. And, of those roughly 21 million kids, 78 percent, or about 16 million, said they were using the internet at school. They are the early adopters and the tech savvy, using their knowledge to access Web 2.0-based content and tools that teachers and parents have no idea exist, and that have little or no value to education.

Sure, most schools have some sort of internet filter to block access to unsafe and inappropriate material, per the Children's Internet Protection Act, which mandates that federally funded schools filter the internet to protect children from online predators, pornography, hate sites, and other unacceptable content while at school. But at Denver Public Schools, we discovered that basic CIPA-compliant technologies, such as rudimentary filters, are not enough. It takes more than just blocking harmful sites to keep students from accessing them.

THE RISKS OF SOCIAL NETWORKING

Making the work of IT administrators harder is that students are interested in less obviously dangerous internet applications such as peer-to-peer programs and sites like MySpace and YouTube. According to top internet tracker Hitwise (http://www.hitwise.com), in July 2006, MySpace received the most hits of any website, accounting for 4.5 percent of all internet visits. A Pew Internet Project report published in January said that more than half of all online American youths ages 12 to 17 use social networking sites. MySpace isn't just an irritant for school IT staff and teachers, who have to constantly check that students aren't wasting school time surfing the site and chatting with friends. The site is sheer trouble. Sexual predators lurk on MySpace and other youth-oriented online communities in search of children who have inadvertently included personal information about themselves, such as where they live, where they work, and where they go to school.

So what's the remedy? Simply blocking access to social networking sites won't suffice. At Denver Public Schools, despite the presence of an internet filtering solution, more than 150,000 attempted visits to MySpace were made in both September and October of 2006. Like most rebellious generations before them, today's tech-smart kids don't take no for an answer, and will often do their very best to surmount the protective wall constructed by school staff to keep them safe. One way they do so is by using anonymous proxies. By configuring their home computers as proxy servers, and then tunneling into them, students can get around a standard filter and gain access to just about any site imaginable. Therefore, it is essential to deploy technology that is able to prevent proxy tunneling and is capable of keeping a record of users who try to evade the filter and access inappropriate sites via proxies and other work-around methods.

Denver's more than 72,000 students and 16,000 computers, dispersed across 120 schools, deepen the need for comprehensive monitoring of staff, teacher, and student school internet use. After careful consideration of many filtering tools, the district chose the R3000 from 8e6 Technologies (http://www.8e6.com). The program's unique proxy pattern blocking keeps users away from sites that offer free anonymous proxy services and prevents them from bypassing the filter if they try to use unencrypted web and client-based proxies.

BEYOND FILTERS

Many IT administrators only focus on the filtering aspect, namely, blocking inappropriate content. But web filters can't stand alone in an effective online safety strategy. At Denver Public Schools, the filter is complemented by a reporting tool that allows administrators to generate individual usage information. By reviewing web logs, DPS can identify trends, react to web usage, and identify the top sites our users are going to. We have instant access to forensic data outlining who was on what sites at what time. Armed with the necessary facts, we can take action when a situation calls for it.

The district doesn't fish for bad behavior; instead we use the reporting tool to respond to requests from teachers and administrators when a child's inappropriate internet use becomes a problem and is in violation of DPS' acceptable use policies. Equally helpful is the tool's ability to generate for every administrator a report that shows the top 25 websites viewed each month in the top 10 categories. The report acts as an indicator of how our students, teachers, and staff are using the internet in school, and helps us set and modify our acceptable internet use policy.

SAFETY FIRST

Like it or not, districts are ultimately responsible for where teachers, staff, and students spend their time online while at school. To protect students from the risks associated with social networking sites, a first step is the creation of an acceptable internet use policy that dictates where each and every constituent is and is not allowed to go online. The most effective policies are those that are created and agreed upon by the administration, understood by the students, and then monitored and enforced by robust filtering and reporting tools.

At Denver, we've also asked parents and teachers to discuss with children the hazards that exist on the internet, and we have coordinated parent and student education programs to address online safety. In addition, the data our reporting tool generates enables us to formulate a comprehensive policy on how to handle our most commonly accessed sites. And we work with teachers and administrators to determine the websites that they most need to be given access to.

No system is fail-safe, particularly when we're operating in territory where the kids are likely to be a step ahead of the adults. But making the safety of the school's online experience a priority can pull us even, and ultimately help us get ahead in the drive toward ensuring our students are safe from the risks and dangers lying in wait on the internet.

Sex Predator[*]

By Asra Q. Nomani
Glamour, December 1, 2007

Dianna Strawder had just stepped out of the shower in the early-morning darkness in July 2006 when her phone rang. It was the roommate of her fiancé, Todd West. "Todd is in jail," he said. All Dianna could sputter out was "What the hell?"

Her head spinning, Dianna couldn't imagine what her sweet, gentle Todd—the man who surprised her on Sunday mornings with Spanish omelets and cried when his cats were sick—had done. But she didn't have time to wonder; she had to get to her job as a medical technician at Loganville Dialysis Center, outside Atlanta, where she would spend the day tending to dialysis patients, hooking them up to the whooshing machines that kept them alive. As she drove to work through the predawn streets, she dialed the Harris County jail and asked the woman at the intake desk what was going on.

"You don't know anything?" the woman said.

"No," Dianna replied.

"Oh, honey," the woman said, "I am *so* sorry."

What the woman told her next made Dianna's hands and knees tremble so hard she had to pull over to the side of the road. Todd had been arrested for trying to solicit sex from a decoy disguised as an underage girl. And Dianna, a 34-year-old divorced mother of two adolescent daughters, was about to endure the private agonies behind what has become a very public form of entertainment.

Her fiancé, she learned, had been caught in a sting orchestrated by the popular *Dateline: To Catch a Predator* series. In the past three years, with the help of an organization called Perverted Justice—a vigilante Internet group whose volunteers pose as children to flush out potential sex offenders—*Dateline* has shown on national television the capture of more than 263 men, many of whom were seeking sex with minors. The stings follow a pattern: A man trolling online for sex exchanges lurid messages with a pseudo-youngster, expressing his interest in hooking up with, for example, a 14-year-old virgin. The decoy then tells the man her parents are away and invites him "home"—to a house outfitted with hidden cameras. When the man arrives, *Dateline* and the police pounce.

Viewers have the satisfaction of seeing these men—who have included public officials, schoolteachers and a rabbi—hauled away, sometimes in handcuffs. But what isn't often shown is the grief and humiliation of those closest to the predators, particularly their wives and girlfriends. And until Dianna Strawder decided to talk to *Glamour*, none of these women had ever spoken to a national magazine.

In the aftermath of the *Dateline* sting, Dianna Strawder has had to wrestle with some disturbing questions. She had to ask herself: Who is this man I said I'd marry? Have I done my daughters irreparable harm? And how will I put our lives back together?

A few days after Todd's arrest, Todd's roommate and Dianna made the drive to the Harris County jail. Furious and confused, Dianna had had just one brief phone conversation with her fiancé since the bust. She'd had time to ask only if he was OK and had no details of what he'd done. As they traveled, the roommate said that a few weeks earlier he and Todd had watched an episode of *Dateline: To Catch a Predator*. The roommate had commented, "I can't believe the freaking idiots who do this kind of thing." He said Todd had nodded his head in agreement.

Their route took them along Interstate 85, the same highway Todd had driven on the way to his planned hookup. As each mile passed, Dianna's anger mounted. Two hours into their trip, near the exit for the decoy house Todd had visited, she finally exploded. "He came all this way!" she exclaimed.

At the jail Dianna stared at Todd through an acrylic window scratched with the words "bitch" and "scumbag." With the visitor's phone held tightly in her hand, she asked him the question that had been gnawing at her: "How old did she say she was?" At first Todd insisted he'd thought the girl he'd met in an online chat room was 18. Then, she says, he hung his head in shame. "Fourteen," he admitted, his voice cracking. Dianna stood up, hurled the phone at the window and stalked out of his sight without saying another word.

On the drive home, Dianna sobbed. Until a few days earlier, she'd trusted Todd more than anyone else in the world. A talented amateur artist who managed a costume shop, he'd always been wonderful with her children. They'd met a little more than a year earlier while standing in line at a Starbucks. "I complimented his boots, and before I knew it, we'd been talking for two hours," she says. "He called a few days later, and we were pretty much together after that." Todd made her feel nurtured, something she'd rarely experienced with a man. "I thought Todd was my soulmate. Getting this news—it was like somebody died."

Now she wasn't sure what to do. Above all was the question of her daughters' safety and well-being; Dianna had custody of her children, and Todd was around the apartment a lot when the girls, ages 11 and 13, were there. There was also the matter of her dignity; Todd had cheated on her in the most humiliating way possible. "I immediately thought about leaving him. I'd decide to do it, and then I'd get sick to my stomach," she says.

Over the next few days, the image of Todd sitting in jail played in her head. But another memory kept surfacing too. When Dianna was 15, she'd been sexually molested by an older man. She'd told her mother, who had confronted the abuser, but charges were never pressed. Dianna couldn't accept that Todd was like this man. "I knew what a sex offender looked like. Todd seemed like the furthest thing from that," she says. "I wasn't OK with what he did, but I wasn't OK with him staying in jail, either."

Dianna decided she'd gather the $7,000 to bail Todd out—but not without trepidation. "I loved Todd, but I wasn't sure about my decision," she says. "I kept asking myself, Am I a lunatic for putting this man near my children?"

While Todd waited in jail, Dianna kept a low profile; outside of Todd's family, the only people who knew what had happened were a few trusted friends. She didn't initially tell her daughters, but later that week, when she picked them up from their father's house, she had to face a question from 13-year-old Rachel. Why, she asked, hadn't Todd been around?

"Todd is in trouble, baby," Dianna replied. "He did a bad thing. He went to visit a girl your age for an indecent purpose."

Rachel fell silent, then asked, "What's that?"

Dianna carefully explained and told her daughters that though she wasn't sure about the future of the relationship, she was going to get Todd out of jail and take him to his home. As Jessica and Rachel sat quietly in the back of the car, it dawned on Dianna how much Todd's arrest would affect them. Her thoughts turned to *Dateline*; their lives would change dramatically when the episode aired in a few months. "The whole world was going to think my girls had a creep for a stepdad. They were going to go to school with that on their shoulders every day," Dianna recalls. Suddenly Rachel broke the silence. "Please don't leave Todd," she pleaded. "You love him, and we love him."

The next night, Dianna posted Todd's bail.

"Thank you," Todd whispered when she arrived. He looked cowed and broken. On the drive to Todd's apartment, Dianna listened to his side of the story. He told her he'd started chatting online with the girl because he was scared of getting married. He hadn't believed she was 14—her language had been too sophisticated, and when he saw her in person, he'd sized her up as being of legal age. (He was right; *Dateline*'s decoys are always 18 or older.) Todd knew he'd made a stupid mistake, he said, but it wasn't anything twisted. He would never, ever do anything bad to a child.

Then Todd told her something that gave her hope: When he'd set out to meet the girl, he said, he'd had second thoughts and turned around. As his car headed in the other direction on the highway, the girl called his cell phone and coaxed him back. Dianna softened. He'd *tried* to do the right thing, she told herself. Maybe he was the man she'd fallen in love with after all. (When *Glamour* asked Perverted Justice about Todd's claim that the decoy lured him back, a spokesperson said, "A decoy will often call the suspect to ensure he's not lost on the way to the home." The organization also said, "That's what [predators] do, they blame everyone but themselves. It comes with the territory of dealing with people who are, at base, uncaring, self-serving individuals more concerned with f—king kids than being decent human beings.")

Dianna felt she knew something about mistakes and redemption. A few years earlier she'd gotten hooked on crystal meth. In 2003 she left her girls with their father while she recovered in rehab. "I've done some rotten things. I've had to ask forgiveness from people—and they've given it," she says. "I believe that people should be able to redeem themselves."

Not everyone felt so generous toward Todd. Friends advised Dianna to leave him, saying that a criminal shouldn't be around her children. Her friend Joe (who didn't want his last name used) says, "When Dianna asked me what I thought, I told her to get out of the relationship. I always thought Todd was nice. I *still* think he's nice. But she has a 13-year-old and an 11-year-old. You just don't put them in that situation." Dianna's ex-husband had similar feelings. When she first told him why Todd was in prison, he exploded, saying, "I don't want that piece of s—t around my kids!" He later calmed down, but he still thought that Dianna should leave Todd. "You deserve better than this," he repeatedly told her.

A month later Dianna finally allowed Todd to see her daughters. Rachel ran up and gave him an enormous hug. He burst into tears. Dianna had a revelation: Todd was part of her family. She felt she had to give him a second chance, even though it wouldn't be an easy choice to live with. Together they'd have to face the repercussions of the broadcast of the *Dateline* episode—and Todd's trial, which would take place sometime early the next year.

That night when she told her girls, they were ecstatic. "I would have been mad if you left him," Jessica told her. "I believe in him." Rachel called Todd, exulting, "Mom says she'll still marry you."

On September 22, 2006, Todd's episode of *Dateline: To Catch a Predator* aired. Dianna and Todd refused to watch it, but in living rooms across the country, 8.7 million viewers heard a voice-over say: "We've hired a young-looking 19-year-old named Amanda to play the part of an underage girl home alone. She gets into position, standing by the front door as a potential predator shows up at our undercover house." The cameras show a man walking up to the front door. The voice-over continues: "Thirty-seven-year-old Todd West has no problem following our decoy right into the house. He's here to meet a girl who online told him she was a 14-year-old virgin. He chatted with the decoy named mystyk_roses for a week."

From there, things only get worse. A blurred image pops up on the screen: It's a shot of Todd's penis, which he sent the girl via webcam. At the *Dateline* house, Todd stands in the kitchen, pouring himself a glass of tea, while the decoy flutters around, asking him if he brought the Jack Daniel's and condoms she'd requested. "Um-hmm," he responds. The camera zooms in on Todd's nervous, smiling face. "Do you have any special ideas for tonight or anything?" the decoy asks. "Not especially," he says. She continues, "What are some of your ideas?" He laughs. "I don't know," he says. "You tell me." That's about as far as Todd gets. After cutting away to another man's story, *Dateline* shows Todd outside the house as cops rush up to him, shouting that he should throw himself to the ground. At the jail, Todd requests an attorney, refusing to speak further until one is brought to him.

Dianna didn't want to get out of bed the next day. Her phone rang endlessly. Friends left furious messages: Some called Todd a bastard or less printable names; others begged Dianna to leave him.

At Jessica's school, people talked about the show—but none seemed to realize Todd's relationship to her mother. In the hallway she heard teachers whisper about the episode, saying, "One of guys even had a fiancée! Can you believe it?" Jessica told her mother that evening at home: "I wanted to tell them how great Todd was."

But in other ways, life remained eerily uneventful. "I kept expecting people to run up to us on the street—to yell at Todd. It never happened," Dianna says. Even so, Dianna felt that Todd was falling apart. When they drove to the movies one evening, he pulled over to cry. "I was trying to live normally, but I had this incredibly depressed person on my hands," says Dianna. "The guilt was eating him alive."

The couple sought counseling from retired Episcopal priest Father R. Dean Johnson and his wife, Anna Johnson, a therapist. Johnson told Dianna, "I don't think this man has any natural propensity to be a child molester."

That insight helped Dianna believe Todd's story about thinking he'd been chatting with an older girl, and as his court date drew nearer, Todd's mental state improved. His public defender was optimistic, saying that considering the types of sentences given to *Dateline* predators, Todd would probably serve a short jail stint. "As crazy as it sounds, our relationship felt stronger than ever," says Dianna. Even Dianna's ex-husband had changed his mind about Todd. "He knew that Todd had acted like an idiot," says Dianna. "But he wasn't a child molester." So when Todd called her one day and asked if she wanted to get married on her lunch break that very afternoon, she said yes.

Dianna expected to feel more settled after their quiet elopement, but the opposite proved true. Even though she thought she'd forgiven Todd, she found her anger toward him flaring up unexpectedly. She couldn't stop obsessing, not just over the repulsive details reported on the *Dateline* episode, but also about his intended infidelity. Every time they walked by a young girl, she glared at him to make sure he wasn't ogling her. More than anything, she worried that her decision to stay with Todd could hurt her girls. She often wondered, Am I the example I want to be?

Three months later there was an additional blow. A grand jury issued a harsh indictment against Todd for his actions: criminal attempt to commit child molestation and criminal attempt to commit statutory rape. In hopes of a light sentence, Todd decided to plead guilty. Father Johnson and his wife testified on Todd's behalf, but the judge wasn't swayed. Sex crimes, said the judge, "are like a computer virus that's out there lurking in cyberspace, at home, looking for young, innocent children." He handed Todd two consecutive 10-year sentences. Because Todd had been arrested in Georgia, where penalties for these crimes tend to be severe, he was given one of the harsher sentences in *Dateline* history. The only bright spot: He could be eligible for parole within a year or two. As the couple left the courthouse, strangers approached Dianna, saying, "We're praying for you."

On the day before Valentine's Day 2007, Todd went to prison.

Life as the wife of a convicted sex predator was relentlessly demoralizing. On her weekly two-hour drives to the prison, Dianna would be greeted by an increasingly fragile and withdrawn Todd. Those few friends who hadn't pulled away from her seemed to scrutinize her too closely. "I could feel them feeling sorry for me," she says.

Her comfort came from her relationship with the community of friends she and Todd had established via MySpace, most of whom didn't know about Todd's crime. Then that changed too. Two weeks after Todd went to jail, a Perverted Justice fan sent an e-mail to Todd's online friends. "This [note] is to inform you that Todd West has been convicted of charges stemming from his arrest in the *Dateline NBC*/Perverted Justice sting operation . . . in which he solicited, for sexual purposes, someone he believed to be 14 years of age," read the e-mail. "While it is never easy to accept that someone you know, even online, has been convicted of such a horrific crime, it is important that you, the general public, be made aware of this serious offense." Included was a link to Perverted Justice's website, which had posted Todd's chat with the *Dateline* decoy. The site poked fun at Dianna. It said, "We're not quite sure who is more deluded . . . Father [Johnson] or the fiancée. Because despite his attempt at 'premarital jitters,' the fiancée married him a month later anyway. . . . Dumb. Dumb. Dumb."

The site also posted a profile about Todd's crime, with links to his e-mail address, IM names and phone number. Every night Dianna and her girls got nasty anonymous phone calls, the mildest of which called Todd a "sicko pervert." Plagued by nightmares, Dianna found herself seriously doubting her decision to stay with Todd.

In her conflicted frame of mind, she began thinking ahead to the next year, when Todd could possibly be out on parole. If he was released as a convicted sex offender, he would have to adhere to a strict set of rules. Dianna didn't remember all the specifics, but she knew that he couldn't be around any books or movies that featured minors. She and the girls decided to do a walk-through of their apartment and make a list of all the things that would have to go when Todd came home. All movies, books and CDs with references to children were banned. *The Addams Family* was out. So were *Aeon Flux*, *Borat* and *The Swiss Family Robinson*. Jessica plucked from the bookshelf one of her favorites from the American Girl Library: *The Care & Keeping of You: The Body Book for Girls* with a cover illustration of three young girls wrapped in bath sheets. "Great," Rachel said. "Minors in towels."

Months later Dianna and her daughters met with Bob Wadkins, Todd's public defender, to discuss Todd's probation restrictions in detail. Soon after they walked into the restaurant, Wadkins said, "You have children. Todd can't live with you." Dianna stared at him, tears blurring her vision. "Can't we appeal?" she asked. "You can make a request to the superior court," said Wadkins, "but there is no judge in Georgia who is going to let your husband live with your daughters."

As the attorney enumerated the rest of the conditions of Todd's probation—no personal photos of minors in the house, no alcohol—Dianna's mind reeled. This was the happiness she was holding out for? A life where Todd could meet her daughters only in public and only if at least six unrelated adults were present?

Dianna confided her dilemma to Todd's roommate. He grimaced. "I love the guy like a brother," he said. "But if I were you, I'd leave him. It's not that I think he was trying to actually have sex with a 14-year-old girl. But this whole mess has become more trouble than it's worth."

In October of this year, Dianna made up her mind to divorce Todd. The two had been married just a year. When she told her daughters of her choice, they were furious. "Rachel didn't say a word to me for two weeks," she says.

But eventually the girls forgave Dianna, though they remain angry at Todd's sentence and upset about the way that *Dateline* tore apart their lives. "If they put this part—the part where the family has to clean up the mess—in the TV show, I don't think the ratings would be nearly as high," Dianna says.

To this day, Dianna believes Todd's story. His arresting officer, Sheriff Mike Jolley, thinks she is deceiving herself: "I've arrested a lot of men like Todd, and I don't believe it's a first time for any of them. There are a lot of frogs who will not turn into princes."

But Dianna is still not convinced that Todd is a sex predator. "I don't believe he is the man that *Dateline* says he is," she says. Her leaving him "is not about Todd being a bad man. It's about me being a good mother." She adds, "I abandoned my kids once when I was addicted to drugs, but I've made a promise to myself never to do that again. They are part of me, my absolute priority. It all comes down to family. This is me keeping that promise."

Survey Finds Teens Solicit Students More Than Adult Predators[*]

School Violence Alert, October 1, 2006

Those concerned about students being sexually solicited online may be confusing adult predator contacts with typical teenage bantering about sex, a Web safety expert says. In the study, Online Victimization of Youth, researchers found student online harassment originates mostly from confrontations at school.

Analysts at The Crimes Against Children Research Center at the University of New Hampshire polled 1,500 students ages 10 to 17 about online harassment. They found sexual solicitations were initiated:

43 percent by other teens.

30 percent by young adults ages 18 to 25.

18 percent by unknown sources.

As a result, researchers urge school administrators to refocus Web safety strategies and program funding on peer harassment. Nancy Willard, director of the Center for Safe and Responsible Internet Use, estimates as many as two-thirds of "so-called sexual solicitations" were from other teens. It's highly likely 8 percent or more of the unknown contacts also came from teens, she says.

While this doesn't minimize the seriousness of adult predation, Willard says officials who fail to distinguish between teen and adult solicitations run the risk of ignoring the bulk of students' online safety threats. She says teens today need to exercise more caution online with acquaintances, not just strangers.

The Online Victimization report compares current trends to those found in a similar 2001 study. Here's what changed:

- Exposure to unwanted sexual material rose from 25 percent to 34 percent despite a 33 to 55 percent increase in the use of filters.
- Online harassment increased from six percent to nine percent.

- Unwanted sexual solicitation dropped from 19 percent to 13 percent.
- Aggressive attempts to contact students offline rose from three percent to four percent.
- Requests for sexually explicit pictures rose from nearly none to three percent.
- Peer harassment increased from three percent to 14 percent.
- Communications with strangers dropped from 40 percent to 34 percent.

Researchers recommend these strategies to help you update your Web safety approach to respond to current trends:

- Aim prevention at teens. Few students under age 12 reported being sexually solicited online. Gear your approach to middle and high school teens. Respect teens' healthy curiosity about sex and acknowledge that they enjoy greater independence than younger students, so don't rely on parental online supervision.
- Talk frankly to teens. Explain how normal adolescent desires for companionship can make teens susceptible to online sexual solicitation. Help students understand this is why it's not a good idea to conduct romances online.
- Caution teens about going online in groups. More students received sexual solicitations or harassed others due to peer pressure in such groups.
- Inform teens about online crime. Tell students about federal child pornography laws that prohibit making and transmitting sexual photography online. Explain it's a crime to take explicit pictures of people under age 18, including themselves.
- Warn teens not to discuss sex with friends online. These transmissions could be reported to police or tracked, and they could be prosecuted.
- Teach teens to report victimization. Instruct students to preserve rather than erase evidence and report sexual solicitation to a trusted adult. Cooperate with law enforcement by learning legal procedures for investigations.
- Explore new technology. Discuss with your school technology director software reporting tools that make it easier for students to report online abuses. Explore offering students privacy settings that help seal off unwanted contacts.

Students reported these types of online victimization:

- Sexual solicitations and approaches. Students were asked to engage in sexual activities or sexual talk. They received requests to provide personal sexual information.
- Aggressive sexual solicitation. Those soliciting students for sex online tried to initiate contact offline through regular mail, by telephone or in person.
- Unwanted exposure to sexual material. Without seeking sexual material online, students were exposed to pictures of naked people or people having sex.

You may view the 2006 report Online Victimization of Youth at www.unh.edu/ccrc/pdf/CV138.pdf.

Lori Drew Is a Meanie[*]

The Problem with Prosecuting Cyber-Bullying

By Emily Bazelon
Slate Magazine, December 23, 2008

As a matter of law, the verdict against Lori Drew in the MySpace suicide case is fairly indefensible. A U.S. attorney in Los Angeles went after a misdeed in Missouri—when state and federal prosecutors there didn't think Drew's actions constituted a crime—with a crazy-broad reading of a statute written to punish computer hacking. Just about every single law professor and editorial writer to weigh in has condemned the prosecutorial overreaching. But the failure to make a valid case against Drew begs a larger question: Is there a better way to go after cyber-bullying? Or is this the kind of troublemaking, however nefarious, the government shouldn't try to punish?

Drew is the mother from hell who famously tried to defend her own teenage daughter against rumor-mongering on the Internet by creating the MySpace persona of fictional 16-year-old Josh Evans, then using that persona to fire off personal e-mail attacks (or sometimes spurring a young woman she worked with to do that). Twenty minutes after "Josh" sent 13-year-old Megan Meier, Drew's daughter's erstwhile friend, the message "the world would be a better place without you," Megan hanged herself in her bedroom.

Someone other than Drew apparently sent that last dreadful e-mail. Even if she had, it seems wrong to say she caused Megan's death. We're talking about an adolescent who must have been vulnerable and volatile and who was taking antidepressants. But the local sheriff's department's dismissal of Drew's MySpace foray as merely "rude" and "immature" doesn't seem proportionate, either. Drew was an adult who secretly entered a teenage world and made it more dangerous. A girl in that world died. The formulation that makes sense to me is that Drew at least contributed to Megan's suicide. So did the abstract verbal brutality of e-mail and the humiliation and shunning made possible by MySpace. But the vacuum cleaner that would cleanse the Web of its pseudonymous nastiness would also suck up a lot of free speech. Freedom often doesn't go with niceness.

The problems with the California case against Drew started with the poor fit between her wrongdoing and the law used to punish her. The federal Computer Fraud and Abuse Act makes it a crime to intentionally access "a computer without authorization." So what does that mean—is it a crime to hack past a password or a firewall? Or merely to violate a terms-of-service contract like the one MySpace users agree to?

In 2003, George Washington University law professor Orin Kerr wrote a prescient law-review article arguing for the former, narrower interpretation. The legislative history for the CFAA indicates that Congress wasn't trying to prosecute any or every breach of contract. Would lawmakers really want to go after people, even potentially, for giving a fake name to register for a Web site, for example (dressed up as the bad act of giving "false and misleading information")? Nor, for that matter, does it look as if Congress intended to base prison time on the MySpace contractual provision that bars use of the site that "harasses or advocates harassment of another person" or that is "abusive, threatening, obscene, defamatory, or libelous." It's one thing for MySpace to kick someone out for acting like a troll or even for the troll's target to sue her. It's another thing entirely to throw the weight of the government behind a criminal investigation and conviction for what usually just amounts to mischief in cyber-contracts.

In the Lori Drew prosecution, the theory was that Drew was on the hook for setting up the fake profile, then using it to inflict emotional distress. Three of the four counts against Drew were for "unauthorized access" of MySpace simply because Drew violated the MySpace terms of service to which she agreed, according to Los Angeles U.S. Attorney Thomas O'Brien's dubious interpretation. The jury didn't think the prosecutors proved the emotional distress and so dismissed the fourth count. And they knocked down the other charges from felonies to misdemeanors. But they did buy the idea that Drew "intentionally" broke the law, even though all that seems to mean is that she clicked "I agree" in response to a long series of legalistic paragraphs that just about nobody really reads. It's hard to imagine even these misdemeanor convictions standing up on appeal.

Kerr joined Drew's defense team, and his post Friday on the Volokh Conspiracy blog gets at how just how ludicrous it is to imagine every breach of a Web site's terms of service as a federal crime. (Kerr: By visiting the Volokh Conspiracy, you agree that your middle name is not Ralph and that you're "super nice." You lied? Gotcha.) Of course, prosecutors aren't really going to investigate all the criminals Kerr just created with the terms of service in his post. But this is not a road we want to take even one baby step down. As Andrew Grossman argues for the Heritage Foundation, laws that make it seem as if "everyone is a criminal" are generally a bad idea. Most of the time, they're unenforceable, and then every once in a while, they're used to scapegoat someone like Lori Drew.

What about a law written expressly to address cyber-bullying? Such a statute could presumably direct prosecutors to go after only the worst of the Internet meanies. Or, then again, maybe not. A proposed bill before Congress is far broader. It targets anyone who uses "electronic means" to transmit "in interstate or foreign commerce any communication, with the intent to coerce, intimidate, harass, or cause substantial emotional distress to a person." The penalty is a fine or imprisonment for up to two years.

Missouri, where Meier lived, has already passed a cyber-bullying law. The Missouri statute extends the state's bar on phone harassment to computers. The problem with the analogy is that the computer context is more dangerous to free speech: On the phone, you talk to one other person. On MySpace or any other Web site, you broadcast to as many people as read you. Other states have passed laws giving schools more authority to address cyber-bullying. That sounds better, but it could get schools too involved in disciplining students for the IMs and posts they write from home.

All of this takes us back to earlier battles over prosecuting hate speech. As Eugene Volokh points out on his ever-vigilant blog, the cyber-bullying bill before Congress is a classic example of a law that's unconstitutional because it's overly broad. The Supreme Court has held that the First Amendment protects "outrageous" speech—from civil as well as criminal liability—even if it "recklessly, knowingly, or purposefully causes 'severe emotional distress,' when it's about a public figure." Volokh adds, "Many, though not all, lower courts have held the same whenever the statement is on a matter of public concern, even about a private figure."

That doesn't mean that a cyber-bullying statute as applied to a Lori Drew-like horror show would be unconstitutional; "Josh's" trashing of Megan was hardly a matter of public concern. But even if a better drafter could come up with a narrower law, since when do we want the government to go after bullies when the only weapon they wield is words? Other countries have experimented with prosecuting hate speech; they don't think their civil traditions are strong enough to withstand, for example, ethnically based calls to violence. But that's not a direction American law has ever taken. And wild and woolly though it may be, the Internet doesn't really call for rethinking our affection for the First Amendment. Cyber-bullying is scary. For some kids, MySpace isn't a safe place. But criminal convictions aren't the best way to clean up the neighborhood.

Decoding MySpace[*]

By Michelle Andrews
U.S. News & World Report, September 18, 2006

Last year, as Margaret Sullivan was reviewing the websites her 13-year-old daughter had visited on the family computer, up popped something called myspace.com. Curious, she clicked on it. "Oh, my God," she thought, as she brought up a page with her daughter's full name, photograph, and school name and location in Wood-Ridge, N.J., along with personal details like her favorite bands and TV shows. "I was so upset," says Sullivan. "All someone had to do to find her was call up the school." At first, her daughter, Shannon, denied knowing anything about the site. "I knew she wasn't going to like what was up there," she says. But Shannon was distressed, too. She couldn't believe her mom was nosing around what she thought was a private place online. "I didn't know everyone could see my page," says Shannon. "I just thought it was a way to talk with my friends."

In the year and a half since Margaret and Shannon had their MySpace confrontation, the social-networking site has exploded in popularity and become the focus of intense parental concern. There are other sites where teens can post profiles and blogs, leave messages for one another, and connect with new people through friends or on their own—sites like Facebook, Xanga, Sconex, Bebo, and Tagged. But MySpace has captured parents' imaginations like no other, and in the worst possible way. To many parents, who may have gotten an eyeful of its sometimes-titillating profiles and photos, MySpace seems like Lake Wobegon gone horribly wrong: a place where all the women are fast, the men are hard-drinking, and the children take an above-average interest in imitating them. How can they allow their kids to roam freely in such an environment? Anyone could be lurking there.

They're right, and to judge from the numbers, it seems that practically everyone is. To join the club, you answer a few questions, upload a photo or two, and voilá, you've got a MySpace profile. Although the site started out as a place for musicians and artists to connect with one another, it has gradually morphed into an online hot spot, and its popularity now easily dwarfs that of others of its kind. The site currently has more than 100 million profiles, with 230,000 new members signing up every day. In August, MySpace accounted for 81 percent of visitors to leading social-networking sites, according to Hitwise, a market-research company. Facebook, a site that's popular with college students, came in a distant second, receiving just 7.3 percent of social-networking traffic. Demonstrating how important these sites are to users, Facebook received scores of angry E-mails last week when it changed some of its features.

Get involved. Among the many millions of people visiting these sites, some, indeed, are sexual predators, and there have been some highly publicized accounts of teenagers who've been lured into offline meetings at which they've been assaulted. Parents, understandably, are traumatized by such stories. By focusing so intently on protecting their kids from stalkers, however, parents have overlooked other less sensational but important aspects of their kids' online experiences. How teens interact with their peers in cyberspace, for example, and how they present themselves through images and words may not be life-or-death decisions, but they can have a serious impact on their lives offline. As the new school year begins, parents have an opportunity to take an interest and get involved in their kids' online experiences, if they haven't done so already.

Even though social-networking sites, instant messaging, chat rooms, E-mail, and the like may not seem to qualify as social gathering spots to parents, for teens, they function very much like the malls and burger joints of earlier eras. They're where young people go to hang out, gossip, posture, dare, and generally figure out how the world works. "What you see is all the behaviors you should recognize from your own teenage years," says Danah Boyd, a doctoral candidate at Berkeley who has studied children's social practices online. "The difference is that now it's less physical and more word-based."

It's also available 24-7. A teenager might check MySpace from home before heading off to school to see if anyone added a comment to his page overnight. Many schools block social-networking sites, but after school, teens often spend hours on them. They'll check their own profiles to see what comments friends may have posted on them, which may be public and available for all the world to read. They may write a few sentences or a couple of paragraphs in their blogs. They'll probably also instant message, or IM, friends to recap the day's events or make plans, upload new photos, or change the music on their page. Then they'll visit their friends' pages to see if they've uploaded any new photos or videos, read new comments from other friends, and post comments of their own. "People have their friends, and now they have the Internet, too," says Matt Zeitlin, a 16-year-old junior in Piedmont, Calif. "It's a more evolved way to communicate than a telephone or cellphone or IM." For some teens, keeping up with their friends online becomes almost an obsession. They compulsively check their messages and look to see who's remarking on their page throughout the day.

Parenting in this virtual world doesn't require a whole new set of skills, though a little technological savvy sure doesn't hurt. What it does require is a willingness to pay attention, ask a lot of questions, and set some rules and stick by them, even at the risk of making your kids mad at you—familiar parenting territory.

"Chicken." But too often that's not happening. Parents who would never allow their child to go to a party unless they knew that an adult would be present let their kids pilot themselves through the online world without any supervision whatsoever. A June survey of 267 pairs of teens and parents in the Los Angeles metropolitan area by a psychology professor at California State University-Dominguez Hills found that two thirds of parents had never talked with their teen about their MySpace use, and 38 percent of them had never seen their child's MySpace profile. "Parents are chicken," says Parry Aftab, an Internet privacy lawyer and executive director of WiredSafety.org, a nonprofit aimed at keeping kids safe online that has trained 450 teenagers in online safety and sends them out to speak to schools and other groups. "They don't understand the technology, so they're reluctant to get involved."

But this is not the time to give in to your inner technophobe. You may have never sent an instant message, uploaded a video, or written a blog, but you can help your kids develop the judgment to better protect their safety online and set standards that will help guide their behavior. This is especially important since legislation that recently passed the House of Representatives and is currently under consideration by the Senate would ban social-networking sites from schools and libraries, leaving parents as the only consistent adult arbiter of their children's day-to-day social-networking behavior.

The problem with the Internet isn't necessarily that sketchy strangers try to entice kids to meet them in person. Strangers approach children on terra firma as well. The problem is that online there are no physical cues to alert a teenage girl that the "boy" who's IMing her about a hot new band is actually a 45-year-old pedophile who's interested in sharing a lot more than his play-list. One of the ways to protect your child is to make sure his or her profile is stripped of identifying details, come-hither photos, and the sort of "I'm lonely" comments that are a red flag for predators (box, below). Another important step is to tackle the issue of making friends online head-on.

Strangers. First, you should understand that "friend" doesn't necessarily have the same meaning on MySpace that it does in the offline world. When your teen creates a profile, Tom Anderson, one of the MySpace founders and a man your child will almost certainly never meet, automatically becomes her first friend, and his name and photo appear on her page. "'Friends' means this is a collection of people I want to pay attention to online," says Boyd. A teen may add a friend because she wants to receive bulletins from this person. Bulletins are announcements someone sends to everyone on his or her list of friends about upcoming parties, for example, or noteworthy events. Or the new pal could be someone who shares a similar interest, such as the same hobby or sport. More troubling, though, some teens accept total strangers as friends in an attempt to boost the total number of friends noted on their page and so appear popular.

Some parents set rules about MySpace friends: MySpace is where you gab with friends you already have, not make new ones. Period. At a minimum, "a parent needs to have a chat with their child about risks," says Larry Magid, coauthor of the new book *MySpace Unraveled: A Parent's Guide to Teen Social Networking*. "People may not be who they say they are; they may be misrepresenting their motives." The wealth of detailed personal information people post online makes social-networking sites fertile ground for predators. While the material may seem innocuous—a home state or a list of favorite TV shows—a predator can use it to his advantage. "The sites help offenders find targets that are close by," says Brad Russ, the former police chief in Portsmouth, N.H., and director of the Internet Crimes Against Children Training and Technical Assistance Program, a Department of Justice effort to help local law enforcement agencies better respond to online sexual exploitation. "One way to break the ice with a child is to become knowledgeable about something that child likes to do," says Russ. Once a child is comfortable E-mailing or IMing the new confidant about, say, who's a favorite on American Idol, conversation easily shifts to more personal topics. Eventually, it won't seem strange to the child if the new pal suggests a face-to-face meeting.

"Non-weird people." MySpace instituted new privacy measures in June to enhance the safety and security of the site. Now, a new feature lets users of any age choose to make their profiles private, so that only friends within their network have access to their personal dossier. In addition, no one over the age of 18 can access a 14- or 15-year-old's profile without knowing the user's full name or E-mail address. Since age verification is impossible, however, these age-based rules are easy to skirt, and many people routinely lie about their age. In fact, MySpace deletes 25,000 profiles weekly of users who don't meet the site's 14-year-old minimum age requirement, says Hemanshu Nigam, chief security officer for the site. The penalty for violators is severe. "We delete them," he says. The profiles aren't the only things that go: Anything posted on other pages disappears as well. Nigam acknowledges the age-based system isn't perfect. "We have considered other ways to set the system up so it is not just about age."

Contrary to parents' perception that their children are easy prey for unscrupulous adults, many kids are just as wary of strangers as their parents or just plain uninterested in meeting them. Zeitlin says he and most of his friends claim to be 14 online. "I do it so people who aren't my friends can't see my profile," he says. "I wouldn't really trust someone online to introduce me to interesting or non-weird people."

According to a new study by the National Center for Missing and Exploited Children, 1 in 7 young people ages 10 to 17 acknowledged receiving an online sexual solicitation in 2005. Five years ago, when the survey was first done, the number was higher: 1 in 5. (Online solicitation is defined as a request to engage in sexual activities or talk or give personal sexual information, from any Internet-based communication.) About 4 percent received "aggressive" solicitations, in which the person wanted to make contact offline, a number that didn't decline from the previous survey.

Dangerous ground. Parents need to be on the lookout, experts say, for unfamiliar friends who contact their children online out of the blue, as well as risky behavior on the part of kids themselves that makes them targets for predators. Too often teens post erotic photos in which they pose suggestively and expose plenty of skin, using screen names like "nasty" or "sexygirl." In their personal description, they may say they're wild or curious about having sex with a stranger. To kids, this may seem like harmless posturing. Parents can help them understand when they're on dangerous ground. "Parents need to talk about certain lines you don't cross," says Magid. "There's a difference between language that's edgy and obscene or profane, and a difference between being sexy and being sexual or slutty."

Some experts worry that while parents focus on sexual predators, however, they miss other ways in which the Internet may be negatively affecting their kids' sexual development. As parents have noticed to their dismay, many kids post very sexualized images of themselves in swimsuits or their underwear. MySpace says it has several staffers who eyeball each of the 3 million images that are posted every day, searching for—and removing—nudity, hate speech or symbols, and offensive content. But photos that are merely provocative aren't forbidden. And with virtually no supervision or monitoring of conversations online, casual banter and egging each other on about sex through online posts and instant messages ("I heard Carmen and Dave hooked up at a party." Response: "No, but he wants to!!!") set the stage for sexual experimentation once kids meet face to face. "Developmentally, the envelope has always been pushed during adolescence," says Sharon Maxwell, a clinical psychologist in Canton, Mass., who specializes in teen sexuality, "but never without any rules. And now it all happens more quickly." This speeding up of sexual development is most pronounced among middle schoolers, Maxwell says.

Just as social-networking sites and Internet communications can accelerate and amplify adolescents' normal sexual explorations, they can do the same with another time-honored teenage tradition: bullying. The old sticks-and-stones nursery rhyme seems quaint now that there's a virtual bathroom wall where kids put all manner of words and images to nasty effect. They may post an unflattering bogus profile claiming a schoolmate is an out-of-control drunk or drug user, with a picture of him passed out at a party, for example, or send scathing text messages among groups of friends when one girl dates someone a friend higher up in the social pecking order is interested in. Dozens of her friends may weigh in—"You're such a whore." "I can't believe you're such a slut."—with instant messages. "Online bullying is more vicious and damaging because it's wider spread," says Nancy Willard, executive director of the Center for Safe and Responsible Internet Use in Eugene, Ore., an education and outreach organization. "More people have access to the communication, and there's the ability to combine damaging images."

The Internet also allows kids to impersonate one another, something that's nearly impossible to do in a school hallway. Last year, five schoolmates at a St. Louis high school decided to post a "hot/not hot" list of more than 100 female classmates, with racist and sexist comments, on Facebook. They signed the name of a 17-year-old junior, who learned of the list only when one of the girls asked him about it. "He was mortified," says Nancy, the boy's mother, who asked to use her first name only. "It was incredibly upsetting, and we were absolutely power-less."

Affirmation. As parents of teenagers are well aware, adolescence is an intensely social time, and now teens can be connected with their peers night and day. Psychologists and Internet experts say they are seeing a growing number of kids who are addicted to being online. Kids who are socially anxious or insecure may be particularly vulnerable, says Willard. Having tons of online friends and being in constant contact through text messaging or cellphones reinforce a feeling of acceptance. But these teens may come to need that hit of affirmation in the brick-and-mortar world to feel OK, she says. Setting limits on the amount of time children can spend online is one obvious strategy, but it's also critical for parents to emphasize the importance of having a balance of interests and activities. This only works, however, if parents themselves have balanced lives and aren't online all the time.

Still, social networking can also be a good thing for some teenagers. "A shy kid who has a terribly hard time expressing himself one-on-one may be much more comfortable conversing online," says Maxwell. Likewise, teens facing difficult issues—gay teens who don't feel comfortable coming out to their parents, for example—can get support online from others in the same situation.

Despite the hand-wringing that teens are spending too many hours online, not every kid is clamoring for a MySpace profile. Elisabeth Moore, a 14-year-old in Stockton Springs, Maine, checked out the site a few months ago and decided not to go back. "It seemed kind of pointless," says Moore, "seeing all these people who don't have much to do except go on the computer. You have your friends in real life; you might as well stick to them."

Common sense. Regular MySpace users, however, can get caught up in sharing their daily dramas and escapades—so engrossed that they sometimes forget the whole world may be watching. There have been many news reports of police nabbing teens who bragged about or posted pictures of their illegal exploits online. Teens in Novato, Calif., for example, got arrested when they posted a video of themselves firebombing an abandoned airplane hangar last spring. More commonplace, however, are photos and postings detailing underage drinking or pot smoking that could conceivably hurt teens' chances when they apply to college or look for a job down the road.

At this time, however, that possibility seems relatively remote. A survey by two counselors at Purdue University's Center for Career Opportunities during the past academic year found that about a third of employers screen job candidates using search engines like Google, while 11.5 percent said that they look at social-networking sites. What's more, colleges don't routinely look at applicants' MySpace or similar profiles. It's a question of time and fairness, says David Hawkins, director of public policy for the National Association for College Admission Counseling. With thousands of applications to review, admissions officers simply don't have time to run names through MySpace. At the same time, "if you look at one person's MySpace profile for something that's not submitted on the application," says Hawkins, "you'd have to look at them all." However, that doesn't mean that employers and admissions officers will turn a blind eye if a problematic profile is brought to their attention. "If a high school counselor said this kid had a MySpace profile that said very negative things about a teacher," Hawkins says, "the admissions officer might consider it."

Many middle schools and high schools currently block social-networking sites on school computers. The Fenn School, a private school in Concord, Mass., for fourth-to-ninth-grade boys, is one of them. School administrators decided that any technology used in the school should serve educational purposes, and MySpace and similar sites don't meet that standard, says Rob Gustavson, the assistant headmaster. At the same time, school administrators believe they have a responsibility to help students develop common sense about their use of technology. One of the segments in the "student life" course, in fact, covers using technology wisely. "We want them to be able to make these judgments when they get outside," says Gustavson. The Deleting Online Predators Act of 2006, which passed the House of Representatives in July, would make blocking of these sites at public schools and libraries mandatory. Although the law's intention is to protect minors from sexual solicitations or suggestive material, many experts believe it is written too broadly and will obstruct many useful sites. And they also argue that banning the sites from the very locations where there are adults present to monitor kids' online activities is a mistake. "If we lock these sites out of the schools, adults are turning their backs on kids and making them deal with these issues on their own," says Henry Jenkins, codirector of the comparative media studies program at the Massachusetts Institute of Technology.

Many experts note that with the proliferation of technology, banning social-networking sites either at school or at home is unlikely to be effective in any case. "The kid will just go underground," says Magid. "You can put a filter on a computer, but you can't prevent him from using it on his cellphone or another computer."

Michelle Alden says she's been tempted to ban MySpace from her house many times. The 40-year-old teacher's aide in Idaho City, Idaho, says she is uncomfortable with the site's profile format, as it encourages youngsters to present themselves as if they're looking for sex. Why, she wonders, does the site ask kids to describe their body type and sexual orientation? But instead of trying to forbid the site, she's opted to set guidelines and talk regularly with her 15-year-old daughter about her page, which she uses primarily to stay in touch with friends. "I think it's better to go ahead and have the struggle, because soon enough she's going to be out on her own," she says, "and I only have a few more years to have those conversations with her."

MySpace may not be your space, but you can help make it a safe place for your teen to hang out.

Online Photos Put Hazing in the Spotlight[*]

By Stacy A. Teicher

The Christian Science Monitor Online, June 14, 2006

The photos are not something that any parent or school official wants to see: college athletes in apparent initiation scenes involving degrading costumes, excessive drinking, sexually suggestive poses with strippers and fellow athletes, and a blindfolded woman with her hands tied behind her back being led down a staircase.

Posted in recent months on Internet sites such as Facebook and BadJocks.com, the photos from more than a dozen colleges are bringing another flurry of attention to hazing rituals. Investigations and disciplinary actions are under way against teams ranging from men's baseball at Elon University in Elon, N.C., to women's soccer at Northwestern University in Evanston, Ill.

The stir is also prompting plans for more-concerted educational initiatives on campuses. The primary goal is to better communicate the dangers of hazing. But it's also another "teachable moment" for students who seem unaware of the damage such online photos can cause to their teams, their schools, and their own future careers.

Despite policies on many campuses and laws in 44 states, antihazing advocates say there hasn't been enough awareness or enforcement. "The prevailing attitude is that hazing has occurred forever, and many coaches, administrators, and even legislators have been hazed and have hazed others, and didn't feel it was such a big deal," says Susan Lipkins, a psychologist in Port Washington, N.Y., and author of the forthcoming book, "Preventing Hazing." In college athletics, she says, the photo postings "really did wake the sleeping giant."

A hazing discussion was added to a meeting of the Pacific-10 Conference in Coeur d'Alene, Idaho, for instance. "Our institutions have a zero-tolerance policy . . . but the recent incidents just reinforce that you need to stay on top of it," says Jim Muldoon, associate commissioner of the Pac-10, whose member schools were not tied to the photos. A committee will consider changing its handbook to address hazing specifically.

"It is a problem that deserves attention and should not be taken lightly," writes Anna Chappell, a star basketball player at the University of Arizona in Tucson and vice chair of the Division I NCAA Student-Athlete Advisory Committee, in an e-mail interview. "I think at times those who are involved with hazing may find it hard to recognize when they might be crossing the line between what is fun and what is dangerous."

Definitions of hazing vary, but generally refer to conduct that is a condition of being in a group and that can cause physical or psychological harm. Many laws and policies say an activity can be deemed hazing even if the subjects give consent.

"The kids call it a head game, and it is—it's about power," Ms. Lipkins says. Older students, who themselves probably underwent initiation, decide it's their turn to take charge, and "they want kids to be blindly obedient and give up their individuality and follow the group."

People who want to stop hazing are up against those who see it as harmless fun or a form of character-building. Among the open-ended comments in a survey of college athletes: "Hazing is a common occurrence that brings a team closer together"; "If no one is hurt to the point that they need medical attention, just leave it alone."

That national benchmark survey, conducted among NCAA athletes in 1998-99 by Alfred University in Alfred, N.Y., found that 79 percent experienced some form of hazing to join a college team. Of those, half said the hazing involved alcohol; two-thirds were subject to humiliation such as being yelled at or forced to wear embarrassing clothes; 1 out of 5 was forced to commit a crime or was subjected to a potentially criminal act such as being kidnapped or tied up and abandoned.

Some schools responded to the recent incidents by prohibiting athletes from participating on photo-sharing Internet sites, *The Chronicle of Higher Education* reports. Others are beefing up orientation to stress to students how to use the sites responsibly.

That has to go hand in hand with asking, "What's going on in the pictures and what can we do to prevent it? Those are the more difficult questions," says Don McPherson, executive director of the Sports Leadership Institute at Adelphi University in Garden City, N.Y. This fall his institute is sponsoring what he says is the first national conference on high school hazing prevention.

At the University of Iowa, a photo of freshmen baseball players surfaced on Facebook, showing them singing at a party in the nude, with baseball caps for fig leaves.

The university concluded that hazing had not taken place. But the photo sparked intense discussions among players, coaches, and faculty. "I can envision scenarios where it could have been hazing, which is why we took it so seriously," says Prof. Elizabeth Altmaier, one of the investigators and a faculty representative to the NCAA.

In separate meetings with freshmen and upperclassmen on the team, they probed to find out whether there was any implication that freshmen were expected to do this to be socially accepted. A group of freshmen chose to do this while others sat out, and several left the party to go to church, with no repercussions, Ms. Altmaier says. She adds that officials clearly conveyed to students that the behavior, including some underage drinking at the party, was unacceptable.

"We're not happy about it, but it could become one of the best educational things for all the student athletes," says the baseball coach, Jack Dahm. Participants felt remorse for making bad choices and attracting negative publicity, he adds. (The photo wasn't posted by a team member.)

Even though this instance wasn't judged to be hazing, Altmaier says, "we have a deep commitment to push back on this topic. . . . There probably are [hazing] rituals that coaches are unaware of."

Lipkins was disappointed with Iowa's ruling. Even "mild" traditions involving voluntary activities that could be deemed embarrassing fit the school's own definition of hazing, she says. The ruling suggests college officials "don't understand the nature of hazing," she says.

Not cracking down can perpetuate a pattern that becomes more severe, but many people don't take the issue seriously until a hazing victim is seriously harmed or dies, antihazing advocates say.

In California, several former fraternity members who served jail time for their role in the death of a pledge, Matthew Carrington, have cooperated in the antihazing work of his mother, Debbie Smith.

"Some of us will go out together and speak—there isn't anything more powerful than that," Ms. Smith says. The young men talk about how close one of them came to calling 911 when it was clear Matt was endangered by being forced to exercise excessively and drink gallons of water. He didn't call because he was discouraged by another fraternity member, Smith says. An hour later when they finally did call, it was too late. "It's like they're brainwashed, and until people understand that's what's happening to our children, it's just going to keep happening," Smith says.

A bill known as "Matt's Law" passed the California Senate and is now moving through the Assembly. It would make hazing a felony if it results in death or serious physical or psychological injury.

ANTIHAZING RESOURCES

www.StopHazing.org (http://www.StopHazing.org) was formed by concerned students and college administrators. With the goal of stopping hazing through education, it provides a wide range of information as well as a discussion forum.

www.InsideHazing.com (http://www.InsideHazing.com) focuses on the psychological aspects of hazing. It is run by psychologist and author Susan Lipkins.

http://hazing.hanknuwer.com is a blog that tracks hazing news and statistics. It's run by Hank Nuwer, a journalist and author.

www.hazing.Cornell.edu (http://www.hazing.Cornell.edu) is run by Cornell University faculty, staff, and student leaders to "examine [hazing] practices explicitly in an attempt to overcome the secrecy that perpetuates them."

5

New Ways of War: Cyberattacks

Editor's Introduction

Cyberwarfare, also known as cyberterrorism, is shaping up to be one of the 21st century's most significant threats. It is a new form of warfare, one that doesn't decimate cities with bombs, but rather renders them inoperable by shutting down their information systems, banks, hospitals, police departments, and other vital infrastructures. Cyberwarfare can be staged by terrorists groups, such as Al-Qaeda, or government organizations. Although the rise of the global Internet has led to advances in commerce, socializing, and other forms of peaceful exchange, it has also made possible new kinds of attacks—ones previous generations couldn't have anticipated.

The selections in this chapter provide an overview of cyberwarfare. In their article "The New E-spionage Threat," Brian Grow and his colleagues shed light on the alarming security problems facing computer systems in the United States. They describe the kinds of cyberattacks that have already been unleashed on U.S. government computer systems, including military networks, and discusses the government's efforts to prevent future incidents.

The second article in the chapter, "When Do Online Attacks Cross the Line Into Cyberwar?," examines the attempts of various governments to define cyberwar. When, or how, should nations be held accountable for sponsoring such attacks? For instance, military officials report that hackers from China have downloaded vast amounts of data from Pentagon computers. The Chinese government denies the allegations, and U.S. officials won't say whether they believe the theft was perpetrated by the Chinese or other hackers. The article attempts to answer the legal implications of these attacks.

The next article, Ian Traynor's "Russia Accused of Unleashing Cyberwar to Disable Estonia," details a 2007 cyberattack launched against Estonia. The attack, which some believe was initiated by the Russian government, came after Estonian officials relocated a Soviet World War II memorial. The assault crippled government, bank, and newspaper Web sites.

In "It's Cyberwar!," Michael Petrou predicts that in the future, Internet attacks will become standard forms of conflict. In particular, he discusses the possibility of an altercation between China and the United States. U.S. officials have speculated that China has been engaging in cyberwarfare, and other governments have voiced the same concern. Worldwide, cyberattacks are increasing at an alarming rate.

In her article "The Flaw at the Heart of the Internet," Erica Naone explains how security researcher Dan Kaminsky identified a "trick" that "could completely break the security of the domain name system and, therefore, of the Internet itself." The next article, "Cybercriminals Can't Get Away With It Like They Used

To," describes how the FBI and Secret Service have cracked down on cybercrime, and how they intend to thwart future attacks. The final piece, "Cyber-Attack Operations Near," by David Fulghum, examines the development of cyberweapons.

The New E-spionage Threat[*]

By Brian Grow, Keith Epstein, and Chi-Chu Tschang
Business Week, April 10, 2008

The e-mail message addressed to a Booz Allen Hamilton executive was mundane—a shopping list sent over by the Pentagon of weaponry India wanted to buy. But the missive turned out to be a brilliant fake. Lurking beneath the description of aircraft, engines, and radar equipment was an insidious piece of computer code known as "Poison Ivy" designed to suck sensitive data out of the $4 billion consulting firm's computer network.

The Pentagon hadn't sent the e-mail at all. Its origin is unknown, but the message traveled through Korea on its way to Booz Allen. Its authors knew enough about the "sender" and "recipient" to craft a message unlikely to arouse suspicion. Had the Booz Allen executive clicked on the attachment, his every keystroke would have been reported back to a mysterious master at the Internet address cybersyndrome.3322.org, which is registered through an obscure company headquartered on the banks of China's Yangtze River.

The U.S. government, and its sprawl of defense contractors, have been the victims of an unprecedented rash of similar cyber attacks over the last two years, say current and former U.S. government officials. "It's espionage on a massive scale," says Paul B. Kurtz, a former high-ranking national security official. Government agencies reported 12,986 cyber security incidents to the U.S. Homeland Security Dept. last fiscal year, triple the number from two years earlier. Incursions on the military's networks were up 55% last year, says Lieutenant General Charles E. Croom, head of the Pentagon's Joint Task Force for Global Network Operations. Private targets like Booz Allen are just as vulnerable and pose just as much potential security risk. "They have our information on their networks. They're building our weapon systems. You wouldn't want that in enemy hands," Croom says. Cyber attackers "are not denying, disrupting, or destroying operations—yet. But that doesn't mean they don't have the capability."

A MONSTER

When the deluge began in 2006, officials scurried to come up with software "patches," "wraps," and other bits of triage. The effort got serious last summer when top military brass discreetly summoned the chief executives or their representatives from the 20 largest U.S. defense contractors to the Pentagon for a "threat briefing." *BusinessWeek* has learned the U.S. government has launched a classified operation called Byzantine Foothold to detect, track, and disarm intrusions on the government's most critical networks. And President George W. Bush on Jan. 8 quietly signed an order known as the Cyber Initiative to overhaul U.S. cyber defenses, at an eventual cost in the tens of billions of dollars, and establishing 12 distinct goals, according to people briefed on its contents. One goal in particular illustrates the urgency and scope of the problem: By June all government agencies must cut the number of communication channels, or ports, through which their networks connect to the Internet from more than 4,000 to fewer than 100. On Apr. 8, Homeland Security Dept. Secretary Michael Chertoff called the President's order a cyber security "Manhattan Project."

But many security experts worry the Internet has become too unwieldy to be tamed. New exploits appear every day, each seemingly more sophisticated than the previous one. The Defense Dept., whose Advanced Research Projects Agency (DARPA) developed the Internet in the 1960s, is beginning to think it created a monster. "You don't need an Army, a Navy, an Air Force to beat the U.S.," says General William T. Lord, commander of the Air Force Cyber Command, a unit formed in November, 2006, to upgrade Air Force computer defenses. "You can be a peer force for the price of the PC on my desk." Military officials have long believed that "it's cheaper, and we kill stuff faster, when we use the Internet to enable high-tech warfare," says a top adviser to the U.S. military on the overhaul of its computer security strategy. "Now they're saying, Oh, shit.'"

Adding to Washington's anxiety, current and former U.S. government officials say many of the new attackers are trained professionals backed by foreign governments. "The new breed of threat that has evolved is nation-state-sponsored stuff," says Amit Yoran, a former director of Homeland Security's National Cyber Security Div. Adds one of the nation's most senior military officers: "We've got to figure out how to get at it before our regrets exceed our ability to react."

The military and intelligence communities have alleged that the People's Republic of China is the U.S.'s biggest cyber menace. "In the past year, numerous computer networks around the world, including those owned by the U.S. government, were subject to intrusions that appear to have originated within the PRC," reads the Pentagon's annual report to Congress on Chinese military power, released on Mar. 3. The preamble of Bush's Cyber Initiative focuses attention on China as well.

Wang Baodong, a spokesman for the Chinese government at its embassy in Washington, says "anti-China forces" are behind the allegations. Assertions by

U.S. officials and others of cyber intrusions sponsored or encouraged by China are unwarranted, he wrote in an Apr. 9 e-mail response to questions from *Business-Week*. "The Chinese government always opposes and forbids any cyber crimes including hacking' that undermine the security of computer networks," says Wang. China itself, he adds, is a victim, "frequently intruded and attacked by hackers from certain countries."

Because the Web allows digital spies and thieves to mask their identities, conceal their physical locations, and bounce malicious code to and fro, it's frequently impossible to pinpoint specific attackers. Network security professionals call this digital masquerade ball "the attribution problem."

A CREDIBLE MESSAGE

In written responses to questions from *BusinessWeek*, officials in the office of National Intelligence Director J. Michael McConnell, a leading proponent of boosting government cyber security, would not comment "on specific code-word programs" such as Byzantine Foothold, nor on "specific intrusions or possible victims." But the department says that "computer intrusions have been successful against a wide range of government and corporate networks across the critical infrastructure and defense industrial base." The White House declined to address the contents of the Cyber Initiative, citing its classified nature.

The e-mail aimed at Booz Allen, obtained by *BusinessWeek* and traced back to an Internet address in China, paints a vivid picture of the alarming new capabilities of America's cyber enemies. On Sept. 5, 2007, at 08:22:21 Eastern time, an e-mail message appeared to be sent to John F. "Jack" Mulhern, vice-president for international military assistance programs at Booz Allen. In the high-tech world of weapons sales, Mulhern's specialty, the e-mail looked authentic enough. "Integrate U.S., Russian, and Indian weapons and avionics," the e-mail noted, describing the Indian government's expectations for its fighter jets. "Source code given to India for indigenous computer upgrade capability." Such lingo could easily be understood by Mulhern. The 62-year-old former U.S. Naval officer and 33-year veteran of Booz Allen's military consulting business is an expert in helping to sell U.S. weapons to foreign governments.

The e-mail was more convincing because of its apparent sender: Stephen J. Moree, a civilian who works for a group that reports to the office of Air Force Secretary Michael W. Wynne. Among its duties, Moree's unit evaluates the security of selling U.S. military aircraft to other countries. There would be little reason to suspect anything seriously amiss in Moree's passing along the highly technical document with "India MRCA Request for Proposal" in the subject line. The Indian government had just released the request a week earlier, on Aug. 28, and the language in the e-mail closely tracked the request. Making the message appear more credible still: It referred to upcoming Air Force communiqués and a "Teaming Meeting" to discuss the deal.

But the missive from Moree to Jack Mulhern was a fake. An analysis of the e-mail's path and attachment, conducted for *BusinessWeek* by three cyber security specialists, shows it was sent by an unknown attacker, bounced through an Internet address in South Korea, was relayed through a Yahoo! server in New York, and finally made its way toward Mulhern's Booz Allen in-box. The analysis also shows the code—known as "malware," for malicious software—tracks keystrokes on the computers of people who open it. A separate program disables security measures such as password protection on Microsoft Access database files, a program often used by large organizations such as the U.S. defense industry to manage big batches of data.

AN E-MAIL'S JOURNEY

While hardly the most sophisticated technique used by electronic thieves these days, "if you have any kind of sensitive documents on Access databases, this [code] is getting in there and getting them out," says a senior executive at a leading cyber security firm that analyzed the e-mail. (The person requested anonymity because his firm provides security consulting to U.S. military departments, defense contractors, and financial institutions.) Commercial computer security firms have dubbed the malicious code "Poison Ivy."

But the malware attached to the fake Air Force e-mail has a more devious—and worrisome—capability. Known as a remote administration tool, or RAT, it gives the attacker control over the "host" PC, capturing screen shots and perusing files. It lurks in the background of Microsoft Internet Explorer browsers while users surf the Web. Then it phones home to its "master" at an Internet address currently registered under the name cybersyndrome.3322.org.

The digital trail to cybersyndrome.3322.org, followed by analysts at *Business-Week*'s request, leads to one of China's largest free domain-name-registration and e-mail services. Called 3322.org, it is registered to a company called Bentium in the city of Changzhou, an industry hub outside Shanghai. A range of security experts say that 3322.org provides names for computers and servers that act as the command and control centers for more than 10,000 pieces of malicious code launched at government and corporate networks in recent years. Many of those PCs are in China; the rest could be anywhere.

The founder of 3322.org, a 37-year-old technology entrepreneur named Peng Yong, says his company merely allows users to register domain names. "As for what our users do, we cannot completely control it," says Peng. The bottom line: If Poison Ivy infected Jack Mulhern's computer at Booz Allen, any secrets inside could be seen in China. And if it spread to other computers, as malware often does, the infection opens windows on potentially sensitive information there, too.

It's not clear whether Mulhern received the e-mail, but the address was accurate. Informed by *BusinessWeek* on Mar. 20 of the fake message, Booz Allen spokesman George Farrar says the company launched a search to find it. As of Apr. 9, says

Farrar, the company had not discovered the e-mail or Poison Ivy in Booz Allen's networks. Farrar says Booz Allen computer security executives examined the PCs of Mulhern and an assistant who received his e-mail. "We take this very seriously," says Farrar. (Mulhern, who retired in March, did not respond to e-mailed requests for comment and declined a request, through Booz Allen, for an interview.)

Air Force officials referred requests for comment to U.S. Defense Secretary Robert M. Gates' office. In an e-mailed response to *BusinessWeek*, Gates' office acknowledges being the target of cyber attacks from "a variety of state and non-state-sponsored organizations to gain unauthorized access to, or otherwise degrade, [Defense Dept.] information systems." But the Pentagon declined to discuss the attempted Booz Allen break-in. The Air Force, meanwhile, would not make Stephen Moree available for comment.

The bogus e-mail, however, seemed to cause a stir inside the Air Force, correspondence reviewed by *BusinessWeek* shows. On Sept. 4, defense analyst James Mulvenon also received the message with Moree and Mulhern's names on it. Security experts believe Mulvenon's e-mail address was secretly included in the "blind copy" line of a version of the message. Mulvenon is director of the Center for Intelligence Research & Analysis and a leading consultant to U.S. defense and intelligence agencies on China's military and cyber strategy. He maintains an Excel spreadsheet of suspect e-mails, malicious code, and hacker groups and passes them along to the authorities. Suspicious of the note when he received it, Mulvenon replied to Moree the next day. Was the e-mail "India spam?" Mulvenon asked.

"I apologize—this e-mail was sent in error—please delete," Moree responded a few hours later.

"No worries," typed Mulvenon. "I have been getting a lot of trojaned Access databases from China lately and just wanted to make sure."

"Interesting—our network folks are looking into some kind of malicious intent behind this e-mail snafu," wrote Moree. Neither the Air Force nor the Defense Dept. would confirm to *BusinessWeek* whether an investigation was conducted. A Pentagon spokesman says that its procedure is to refer attacks to law enforcement or counterintelligence agencies. He would not disclose which, if any, is investigating the Air Force e-mail.

DIGITAL INTRUDERS

By itself, the bid to steal digital secrets from Booz Allen might not be deeply troubling. But Poison Ivy is part of a new type of digital intruder rendering traditional defenses—firewalls and updated antivirus software—virtually useless. Sophisticated hackers, say Pentagon officials, are developing new ways to creep into computer networks sometimes before those vulnerabilities are known. "The offense has a big advantage over the defense right now," says Colonel Ward E. Heinke, director of the Air Force Network Operations Center at Barksdale Air Force

Base. Only 11 of the top 34 antivirus software programs identified Poison Ivy when it was first tested on behalf of *BusinessWeek* in February. Malware-sniffing software from several top security firms found "no virus" in the India fighter-jet e-mail, the analysis showed.

Over the past two years thousands of highly customized e-mails akin to Stephen Moree's have landed in the laptops and PCs of U.S. government workers and defense contracting executives. According to sources familiar with the matter, the attacks targeted sensitive information on the networks of at least seven agencies—the Defense, State, Energy, Commerce, Health & Human Services, Agriculture, and Treasury departments—and also defense contractors Boeing, and General Dynamics, say current and former government network security experts. Laura Keehner, a spokeswoman for the Homeland Security Dept., which coordinates protection of government computers, declined to comment on specific intrusions. In written responses to questions from *BusinessWeek*, Keehner says: "We are aware of and have defended against malicious cyber activity directed at the U.S. Government over the past few years. We take these threats seriously and continue to remain concerned that this activity is growing more sophisticated, more targeted, and more prevalent." Spokesmen for Lockheed Martin, Boeing, Raytheon, General Dynamics, and General Electric declined to comment. Several cited policies of not discussing security-related matters.

The rash of computer infections is the subject of Byzantine Foothold, the classified operation designed to root out the perpetrators and protect systems in the future, according to three people familiar with the matter. In some cases, the government's own cyber security experts are engaged in "hack-backs"—following the malicious code to peer into the hackers' own computer systems. *BusinessWeek* has learned that a classified document called an intelligence community assessment, or ICA, details the Byzantine intrusions and assigns each a unique Byzantine-related name. The ICA has circulated in recent months among selected officials at U.S. intelligence agencies, the Pentagon, and cyber security consultants acting as outside reviewers. Until December, details of the ICA's contents had not even been shared with congressional intelligence committees.

Now, Senate Intelligence Committee Chairman John D. Rockefeller (D-W. Va.) is said to be discreetly informing fellow senators of the Byzantine operation, in part to win their support for needed appropriations, many of which are part of classified "black" budgets kept off official government books. Rockefeller declined to comment. In January a Senate Intelligence Committee staffer urged his boss, Missouri Republican Christopher "Kit" Bond, the committee's vice-chairman, to supplement closed-door testimony and classified documents with a viewing of the movie Die Hard 4 on a flight the senator made to New Zealand. In the film, cyber terrorists breach FBI networks, purloin financial data, and bring car traffic to a halt in Washington. Hollywood, says Bond, doesn't exaggerate as much as people might think. "I can't discuss classified matters," he cautions. "But the movie illustrates the potential impact of a cyber conflict. Except for a few things, let me just tell you: It's credible."

"Phishing," one technique used in many attacks, allows cyber spies to steal information by posing as a trustworthy entity in an online communication. The term was coined in the mid-1990s when hackers began "fishing" for information (and tweaked the spelling). The e-mail attacks on government agencies and defense contractors, called "spear-phish" because they target specific individuals, are the Web version of laser-guided missiles. Spear-phish creators gather information about people's jobs and social networks, often from publicly available information and data stolen from other infected computers, and then trick them into opening an e-mail.

DEVIOUS SCRIPT

Spear-phish tap into a cyber espionage tactic that security experts call "Net reconnaissance." In the attempted attack on Booz Allen, attackers had plenty of information about Moree: his full name, title (Northeast Asia Branch Chief), job responsibilities, and e-mail address. Net reconnaissance can be surprisingly simple, often starting with a Google search. (A lookup of the Air Force's Pentagon e-mail address on Apr. 9, for instance, retrieved 8,680 e-mail addresses for current or former Air Force personnel and departments.) The information is woven into a fake e-mail with a link to an infected Web site or containing an attached document. All attackers have to do is hit their send button. Once the e-mail is opened, intruders are automatically ushered inside the walled perimeter of computer networks—and malicious code such as Poison Ivy can take over.

By mid-2007 analysts at the National Security Agency began to discern a pattern: personalized e-mails with corrupted attachments such as PowerPoint presentations, Word documents, and Access database files had been turning up on computers connected to the networks of numerous agencies and defense contractors.

A previously undisclosed breach in the autumn of 2005 at the American Enterprise Institute—a conservative think tank whose former officials and corporate executive board members are closely connected to the Bush Administration-proved so nettlesome that the White House shut off aides' access to the Web site for more than six months, says a cyber security specialist familiar with the incident. The Defense Dept. shut the door for even longer. Computer security investigators, one of whom spoke with *BusinessWeek*, identified the culprit: a few lines of Java script buried in AEI's home page, www.aei.org, that activated as soon as someone visited the site. The script secretly redirected the user's computer to another server that attempted to load malware. The malware, in turn, sent information from the visitor's hard drive to a server in China. But the security specialist says cyber sleuths couldn't get rid of the intruder. After each deletion, the furtive code would reappear. AEI says otherwise—except for a brief accidental recurrence caused by its own network personnel in August, 2007, the devious Java script did not return and was not difficult to eradicate.

The government has yet to disclose the breaches related to Byzantine Foothold. *BusinessWeek* has learned that intruders managed to worm into the State Dept.'s highly sensitive Bureau of Intelligence & Research, a key channel between the work of intelligence agencies and the rest of the government. The breach posed a risk to CIA operatives in embassies around the globe, say several network security specialists familiar with the effort to cope with what became seen as an internal crisis. Teams worked around-the-clock in search of malware, they say, calling the White House regularly with updates.

The attack began in May, 2006, when an unwitting employee in the State Dept.'s East Asia Pacific region clicked on an attachment in a seemingly authentic e-mail. Malicious code was embedded in the Word document, a congressional speech, and opened a Trojan "back door" for the code's creators to peer inside the State Dept.'s innermost networks. Soon, cyber security engineers began spotting more intrusions in State Dept. computers across the globe. The malware took advantage of previously unknown vulnerabilities in the Microsoft operating system. Unable to develop a patch quickly enough, engineers watched helplessly as streams of State Dept. data slipped through the back door and into the Internet ether. Although they were unable to fix the vulnerability, specialists came up with a temporary scheme to block further infections. They also yanked connections to the Internet.

One member of the emergency team summoned to the scene recalls that each time cyber security professionals thought they had eliminated the source of a "beacon" reporting back to its master, another popped up. He compared the effort to the arcade game Whack-A-Mole. The State Dept. says it eradicated the infection, but only after sanitizing scores of infected computers and servers and changing passwords. Microsoft's own patch, meanwhile, was not deployed until August, 2006, three months after the infection. A Microsoft spokeswoman declined to comment on the episode, but said: "Microsoft has, for several years, taken a comprehensive approach to help protect people online."

There is little doubt among senior U.S. officials about where the trail of the recent wave of attacks leads. "The Byzantine series tracks back to China," says Air Force Colonel Heinke. More than a dozen current and former U.S. military, cyber security, and intelligence officials interviewed by *BusinessWeek* say China is the biggest emerging adversary—and not just clubs of rogue or enterprising hackers who happen to be Chinese. O. Sami Saydjari, a former National Security Agency executive and now president of computer security firm Cyber Defense Agency, says the Chinese People's Liberation Army, one of the world's largest military forces, with an annual budget of $57 billion, has "tens of thousands" of trainees launching attacks on U.S. computer networks. Those figures could not be independently confirmed by *BusinessWeek*. Other experts provide lower estimates and note that even one hacker can do a lot of damage. Says Saydjari: "We have to look at this as equivalent to the launch of a Chinese Sputnik." China vigorously disputes the spying allegation and says its military posture is purely defensive.

Hints of the perils perceived within America's corridors of power have been slipping out in recent months. In Feb. 27 testimony before the U.S. Senate Armed Services Committee, National Intelligence Director McConnell echoed the view that the threat comes from China. He told Congress he worries less about people capturing information than altering it. "If someone has the ability to enter information in systems, they can destroy data. And the destroyed data could be something like money supply, electric-power distribution, transportation sequencing, and that sort of thing." His conclusion: "The federal government is not well-protected and the private sector is not well-protected."

Worries about China-sponsored Internet attacks spread last year to Germany, France, and Britain. British domestic intelligence agency MI5 had seen enough evidence of intrusion and theft of corporate secrets by allegedly state-sponsored Chinese hackers by November, 2007, that the agency's director general, Jonathan Evans, sent an unusual letter of warning to 300 corporations, accounting firms, and law firms—and a list of network security specialists to help block computer intrusions. Some recipients of the MI5 letter hired Peter Yapp, a leading security consultant with London-based Control Risks. "People treat this like it's just another hacker story, and it is almost unbelievable," says Yapp. "There's a James Bond element to it. Too many people think, It's not going to happen to me.' But it has."

Identifying the thieves slipping their malware through the digital gates can be tricky. Some computer security specialists doubt China's government is involved in cyber attacks on U.S. defense targets. Peter Sommer, an information systems security specialist at the London School of Economics who helps companies secure networks, says: "I suspect if it's an official part of the Chinese government, you wouldn't be spotting it."

A range of attacks in the past two years on U.S. and foreign government entities, defense contractors, and corporate networks have been traced to Internet addresses registered through Chinese domain name services such as 3322.org, run by Peng Yong. In late March, *BusinessWeek* interviewed Peng in an apartment on the 14th floor of the gray-tiled residential building that houses the five-person office for 3322.org in Changzhou. Peng says he started 3322.org in 2001 with $14,000 of his own money so the growing ranks of China's Net surfers could register Web sites and distribute data. "We felt that this business would be very popular, especially as broadband, fiber-optic cables, [data transmission technology] ADSL, these ways of getting on the Internet took off," says Peng (translated by *Business-Week* from Mandarin), who drives a black Lexus IS300 bought last year.

His 3322.org has indeed become a hit. Peng says the service has registered more than 1 million domain names, charging $14 per year for "top-level" names ending in .com, .org, or .net. But cyber security experts and the Homeland Security Dept.'s U.S. Computer Emergency Readiness Team (CERT) say that 3322.org is a hit with another group: hackers. That's because 3322.org and five sister sites controlled by Peng are dynamic DNS providers. Like an Internet phone book, dynamic DNS assigns names for the digits that mark a computer's location on the

Web. For example, 3322.org is the registrar for the name cybersyndrome.3322.org at Internet address 61.234.4.28, the China-based computer that was contacted by the malicious code in the attempted Booz Allen attack, according to analyses reviewed by *BusinessWeek*. "Hackers started using sites like 3322.org so that the malware phones home to the specific name. The reason? It is relatively difficult to have [Internet addresses] taken down in China," says Maarten van Horenbeeck, a Belgium-based intrusion analyst for the SANS Internet Storm Center, a cyber threat monitoring group.

TARGET: PRIVATE SECTOR

Peng's 3322.org and sister sites have become a source of concern to the U.S. government and private firms. Cyber security firm Team Cymru sent a confidential report, reviewed by *BusinessWeek*, to clients on Mar. 7 that illustrates how 3322.org has enabled many recent attacks. In early March, the report says, Team Cymru received "a spoofed e-mail message from a U.S. military entity, and the PowerPoint attachment had a malware widget embedded in it." The e-mail was a spear-phish. The computer that controlled the malicious code in the PowerPoint? Cybersyndrome.3322.org—the same China-registered computer in the attempted attack on Booz Allen. Although the cybersyndrome Internet address may not be located in China, the top five computers communicating directly with it were—and four were registered with a large state-owned Internet service provider, according to the report.

A person familiar with Team Cymru's research says the company has 10,710 distinct malware samples that communicate to masters registered through 3322.org. Other groups reporting attacks from computers hosted by 3322.org include activist group Students for a Free Tibet, the European Parliament, and U.S. Bancorp, according to security reports. Team Cymru declined to comment. The U.S. government has pinpointed Peng's services as a problem, too. In a Nov. 28, 2007, confidential report from Homeland Security's U.S. CERT obtained by *Business-Week*, "Cyber Incidents Suspected of Impacting Private Sector Networks," the federal cyber watchdog warned U.S. corporate information technology staff to update security software to block Internet traffic from a dozen Web addresses after spear-phishing attacks. "The level of sophistication and scope of these cyber security incidents indicates they are coordinated and targeted at private-sector systems," says the report. Among the sites named: Peng's 3322.org, as well as his 8800.org, 9966.org, and 8866.org. Homeland Security and U.S. CERT declined to discuss the report.

Peng says he has no idea hackers are using his service to send and control malicious code. "Are there a lot?" he says when asked why so many hackers use 3322.org. He says his business is not responsible for cyber attacks on U.S. computers. "It's like we have paved a road and what sort of car [users] drive on it is their own business," says Peng, who adds that he spends most of his time these days developing Internet telephony for his new software firm, Bitcomm Software Tech Co. Peng says he was not aware that several of his Web sites and Internet addresses registered through them were named in the U.S. CERT report. On Apr. 7, he said he planned to shut the sites down and contact the U.S. agency. Asked by *Business-Week* to check his database for the person who registered the computer at the domain name cybersyndrome.3322.org, Peng says it is registered to Gansu Railway Communications, a regional telecom subsidiary of China's Railways Ministry. Peng declined to provide the name of the registrant, citing a confidentiality agreement. "You can go through the police to find out the user information," says Peng.

U.S. cyber security experts say it's doubtful that the Chinese government would allow the high volume of attacks on U.S. entities from China-based computers if it didn't want them to happen. "China has one of the best-controlled Internets in the world. Anything that happens on their Internet requires permission," says Cyber Defense Group's Saydjari. The Chinese government spokesman declined to answer specific questions from *BusinessWeek* about 3322.org.

But Peng says he can do little if hackers exploit his goodwill—and there hasn't been much incentive from the Chinese government for him to get tough. "Normally, we take care of these problems by shutting them down," says Peng. "Because our laws do not have an extremely clear method to handle this problem, sometimes we are helpless to stop their services." And so, it seems thus far, is the U.S. government.

When Do Online Attacks Cross the Line Into Cyberwar?*

By Alex Kingsbury

U.S. News & World Report, December 9, 2008

The international community urgently needs to establish legal norms when it comes to computer and online crimes to help define and deter a problem that is escalating in severity, cyber security experts say.

A bipartisan commission examining the nation's cybersecurity infrastructure concluded this week that the next president needs to clearly articulate the value of the nation's cyber domain. Of course, many groups are already looking at the issue, from NATO, which is focused on military applications, and the Department of Homeland Security to the European Union.

But the commission urged action from the White House directly. "The president should state as a fundamental principle that cyberspace is a vital asset for the nation and that the United States will protect it using all instruments of national power, in order to ensure national security, public safety, economic prosperity, and the delivery of critical services to the American public."

Of course, just the act of codifying cyberattacks, cybercrimes, or cyberwar would do little to physically prevent them from happening, says Jonathan Zittrain, a law professor at Harvard University and author of *The Future of the Internet and How to Stop It*. But it could have a deterrent effect, establishing a legal basis for punishing states that sponsor such incidents.

Two years ago, military officials reported that China had downloaded between 10 and 20 terabytes of information from Pentagon computers—a volume of data equivalent to twice the number of printed pages in the Library of Congress. The Chinese government has routinely denied all allegations of espionage, and Pentagon officials aren't saying if they believed the Chinese government or simply hackers based in or routed through China were responsible.

In many countries, breaking into a computer network and copying files is no different from physically stealing paper documents from an office desk. But could such cyberattacks be considered an act of war, equivalent to attacking a pair of destroyers off the coast of Asia or striking a group of battle ships at anchor in Hawaii?

The U.S. military, meanwhile, lacks a formal doctrine on offensive military operations in cyberspace, although the Bush administration is "racing" to finalize such a policy before it leaves office, says one person familiar with the White House's work on the issue.

In the past few years, there has been a flood of attacks against U.S. computer assets, including classified and unclassified military networks and business and commerce sites, not to mention personal computers. Coordinated cyberattacks against Georgia, which coincided with Russian military action, and Estonia have raised even more concerns about what role cyberattacks could play in future conflicts.

Online assaults have also been mounted against America's enemies, including al Qaeda. For days before the anniversary of the 9/11 attacks this year, coordinated attacks were carried out against several websites known for posting messages from al Qaeda's leadership. Al Qaeda's anniversary message did eventually make its way onto the Net, but only days later.

No one claimed responsibility for the al Qaeda site attacks, and they could have simply been the work of vigilante computer experts, hackers, or other players entirely.

That's another vexing aspect of cyberattacks—they are often conducted across multiple national borders, making it very difficult to affix blame. For instance, some of the computers used (unwittingly) in the cyberattacks against Georgia were based in the United States, among other places, computer security experts say.

There are three central issues with which the international legal community must grapple as the debate continues, says James Lewis, the project director of the Commission on Cybersecurity of the 44th Presidency, which issued its report this week. Each country might have different answers, but the questions will be universal.

- At what point does a cyberattack constitute an act of war or a violation severe enough to justify a response?
- How do we protect the civil liberties of the Internet-using public while improving security?
- Which legal authorities will assume responsibility for investigating a cyberattack—the intelligence community, the military, or law enforcement?

The debate over codifying cyberattacks, Lewis points out, echoes some debates over terrorism, including whether it should primarily be a law enforcement or military concern and how to respond to attacks by state-sponsored actors.

Russia Accused of Unleashing Cyberwar to Disable Estonia*

By Ian Traynor
The Guardian, May 17, 2007

A three-week wave of massive cyber-attacks on the small Baltic country of Estonia, the first known incidence of such an assault on a state, is causing alarm across the western alliance, with Nato urgently examining the offensive and its implications.

While Russia and Estonia are embroiled in their worst dispute since the collapse of the Soviet Union, a row that erupted at the end of last month over the Estonians' removal of the Bronze Soldier Soviet war memorial in central Tallinn, the country has been subjected to a barrage of cyber warfare, disabling the websites of government ministries, political parties, newspapers, banks, and companies.

Nato has dispatched some of its top cyber-terrorism experts to Tallinn to investigate and to help the Estonians beef up their electronic defences.

"This is an operational security issue, something we're taking very seriously," said an official at Nato headquarters in Brussels. "It goes to the heart of the alliance's modus operandi."

Alarm over the unprecedented scale of cyber-warfare is to be raised tomorrow at a summit between Russian and European leaders outside Samara on the Volga.

While planning to raise the issue with the Russian authorities, EU and Nato officials have been careful not to accuse the Russians directly.

If it were established that Russia is behind the attacks, it would be the first known case of one state targeting another by cyber-warfare.

Relations between the Kremlin and the west are at their worst for years, with Russia engaged in bitter disputes not only with Estonia, but with Poland, Lithuania, the Czech Republic, and Georgia—all former parts of the Soviet Union or ex-members of the Warsaw Pact. The electronic offensive is making matters much worse.

"Frankly it is clear that what happened in Estonia in the cyber-attacks is not acceptable and a very serious disturbance," said a senior EU official.

Estonia's president, foreign minister, and defence minister have all raised the emergency with their counterparts in Europe and with Nato.

"At present, Nato does not define cyber-attacks as a clear military action. This means that the provisions of Article V of the North Atlantic Treaty, or, in other words collective self-defence, will not automatically be extended to the attacked country," said the Estonian defence minister, Jaak Aaviksoo.

"Not a single Nato defence minister would define a cyber-attack as a clear military action at present. However, this matter needs to be resolved in the near future."

Estonia, a country of 1.4 million people, including a large ethnic Russian minority, is one of the most wired societies in Europe and a pioneer in the development of "e-government". Being highly dependent on computers, it is also highly vulnerable to cyber-attack.

The main targets have been the websites of:
- the Estonian presidency and its parliament
- almost all of the country's government ministries
- political parties
- three of the country's six big news organisations
- two of the biggest banks; and firms specializing in communications

It is not clear how great the damage has been.

With their reputation for electronic prowess, the Estonians have been quick to marshal their defences, mainly by closing down the sites under attack to foreign internet addresses, in order to try to keep them accessible to domestic users.

The cyber-attacks were clearly prompted by the Estonians' relocation of the Soviet second world war memorial on April 27.

Ethnic Russians staged protests against the removal, during which 1,300 people were arrested, 100 people were injured, and one person was killed.

The crisis unleashed a wave of so-called DDoS, or Distributed Denial of Service, attacks, where websites are suddenly swamped by tens of thousands of visits, jamming and disabling them by overcrowding the bandwidths for the servers running the sites. The attacks have been pouring in from all over the world, but Estonian officials and computer security experts say that, particularly in the early phase, some attackers were identified by their internet addresses - many of which were Russian, and some of which were from Russian state institutions.

"The cyber-attacks are from Russia. There is no question. It's political," said Merit Kopli, editor of Postimees, one of the two main newspapers in Estonia, whose website has been targeted and has been inaccessible to international visitors for a week. It was still unavailable last night.

"If you are implying [the attacks] came from Russia or the Russian government, it's a serious allegation that has to be substantiated. Cyber-space is everywhere," Russia's ambassador in Brussels, Vladimir Chizhov, said in reply to a question from the Guardian. He added: "I don't support such behaviour, but one has to look at where they [the attacks] came from and why."

Without naming Russia, the Nato official said: "I won't point fingers. But these were not things done by a few individuals.

"This clearly bore the hallmarks of something concerted. The Estonians are not alone with this problem. It really is a serious issue for the alliance as a whole."

Mr Chizhov went on to accuse the EU of hypocrisy in its support for Estonia, an EU and Nato member. "There is a smell of double standards."

He also accused Poland of holding the EU hostage in its dealings with Russia, and further accused Estonia and other east European countries previously in Russia's orbit of being in thrall to "phantom pains of the past, historic grievances against the Soviet union and the Russian empire of the 19th century." In Tallinn, Ms Kopli said: "This is the first time this has happened, and it is very important that we've had this type of attack. We've been able to learn from it."

"We have been lucky to survive this," said Mikko Maddis, Estonia's defence ministry spokesman. "People started to fight a cyber-war against it right away. Ways were found to eliminate the attacker."

The attacks have come in three waves: from April 27, when the Bronze Soldier riots erupted, peaking around May 3; then on May 8 and 9—a couple of the most celebrated dates in the Russian calendar, when the country marks Victory Day over Nazi Germany, and when President Vladimir Putin delivered another hostile speech attacking Estonia and indirectly likening the Bush administration to the Hitler regime; and again this week.

Estonian officials say that one of the masterminds of the cyber-campaign, identified from his online name, is connected to the Russian security service. A 19-year-old was arrested in Tallinn at the weekend for his alleged involvement.

Expert opinion is divided on whether the identity of the cyber-warriors can be ascertained properly.

Experts from Nato member states and from the alliance's NCSA unit—"Nato's first line of defence against cyber-terrorism", set up five years ago—were meeting in Seattle in the US when the crisis erupted. A couple of them were rushed to Tallinn.

Another Nato official familiar with the experts' work said it was easy for them, with other organisations and internet providers, to track, trace, and identify the attackers.

But Mikko Hyppoenen, a Finnish expert, told the Helsingin Sanomat newspaper that it would be difficult to prove the Russian state's responsibility, and that the Kremlin could inflict much more serious cyber-damage if it chose to.

It's Cyberwar!*

Web Attacks May Soon Become a Standard Part of Global Conflicts

By Michael Petrou
Maclean's, October 15, 2007

In the overheated rhetoric of Chinese military strategists, it is known as the assassin's mace—an expression that refers to an unconventional weapon or strategy whose impact is so unexpected and unpredictable that it can tilt the balance of war in favour of the weaker combatant. The Chinese assassin's primary target is the United States. The assassin's weapon, however, relies more on intrigue and technological sabotage than brute force. Earlier this month, American officials, speaking off the record to the Financial Times, disclosed that hackers connected to the Chinese People's Liberation Army had successfully penetrated a Pentagon computer network. The online raid offered a glimpse into the growing importance of cyberwarfare, China's newest assassin's mace.

Germany has also accused the People's Liberation Army of hacking into its networks, and Britain admits that attempts to penetrate its networked systems are a growing problem. In fact, most developed countries are widely assumed to engage in cyberespionage, which refers to the extraction of sensitive information from the networked systems of governments and private businesses—accomplishing what traditional spies once did without the trouble of risking capture, or straying far from a computer terminal. "That's the beauty of the Internet," says James Lewis, a senior fellow at the Center for Strategic & International Studies in Washington. "Twenty years ago, you had to send somebody to skulk around in bars outside the plant gates and hope you could recruit someone. Now you can do it remotely."

Cyberwarfare is a step beyond espionage. It involves disabling or corrupting an adversary's computer systems. This spring, for example, Estonia accused Russia of cyberattacks that crippled bank and government computers following a dispute between the two nations about a Russian war memorial in the Estonian capital. Russia has also been accused of cyberattacks against Ukraine, while South Korea has alleged that North Korea has trained 600 hackers for attacks not only against it but also the U.S. and Japan.

It is China that is the most aggressive—and perhaps least discreet—about its efforts to exploit cyberwarfare's potential. This is because cyberattacks are seen as valuable weapons in asymmetric warfare, meaning a contest between unevenly matched opponents. "China is convinced that, financially and technologically, it cannot defeat the United States in a traditional force-on-force matchup," reported the U.S.-China Economic and Security Review Commission in testimony to Congress this June. "As evidenced by the trajectory of its military modernization, Chinese defence planners are seeking to accomplish the goal of undermining the U.S. military's technological edge through a variety of disruptive means. Among these is cyberwarfare."

The cyberwarfare envisioned by the Chinese would entail more than the on-line vandalism directed against Estonia. Some analysts point to what James Lewis calls the "Godzilla scenario," in which a country's entire infrastructure is targeted, banks, airports and communications networks are shut down, and public order disintegrates. The chances of such a scenario unfolding are remote. It is unlikely that the Chinese, or any other state, have the capability to unleash such damage, and doing so would only be useful in a total war.

A real conflict between China and the United States, however, would almost certainly be a limited one fought over Taiwan, an American ally that China views as a breakaway province to be "reunified" with the rest of China. The United States has pledged to assist Taiwan should China invade. But geography favours the Chinese. Taiwan lies just off the coast of China but is separated from the United States by the Pacific Ocean. In any war with China, Taiwan's strategy will be to hold out until U.S. forces arrive. China's strategy is to delay that arrival long enough to force Taiwan to negotiate its capitulation.

James Mulvenon, director of the Center for Intelligence Research and Analysis, which does contract research for the American intelligence community and the Department of Defense, says that the Chinese have probed American military networks and concluded that attacking them can cause the most damage when forces are being marshalled and sent to a conflict zone. "If you allow the U.S. military to get locked and loaded on your border with the full-force protection package, it's over," he said in an interview with *Maclean's*. "The U.S. military is just going to pick apart your command and control network, and it's going to be ugly. But the vulnerability is in that deployment phase."

Cyberattacks are not going to win a war on their own. "The problem for the Chinese is, right now there is no way they can use cyberweapons to stop carrier battle groups from leaving California and going to Taiwan," James Lewis says. "But suppose you could distort the information that your opponent's commanders were receiving. Suppose you could distort GPS signals, data, email, the whole bit, so that they distrusted the information they were getting. If you can do that, if you can create uncertainty in the minds of your opponents, then you've got an advantage."

The United States clearly believes the threat presented by cyberwarfare is real. It will establish a "Cyber Command," to be run by the U.S. Air Force, which, according to Maj.-Gen. Charles Ickes, will "train and equip forces to conduct sustained global operations in and through cyberspace, fully integrated with air and space operations." The Department of Homeland Security also has a cybersecurity division to protect civilian networks.

For the moment, these are precautions against a threat that is not yet fully developed. "It's still a form of warfare that is over the horizon," says Wesley Wark, a visiting research professor at the University of Ottawa who specializes in intelligence and security issues. Of course, the same might once have been said about countless other military innovations, from gunpowder to mechanized flight.

The Flaw at the Heart of the Internet[*]

By Erica Naone

Technology Review (Cambridge Mass.), November/December 2008

Dan Kaminsky, uncharacteristically, was not looking for bugs earlier this year when he happened upon a flaw at the core of the Internet. The security researcher was using his knowledge of Internet infrastructure to come up with a better way to stream videos to users. Kaminsky's expertise is in the Internet's domain name system (DNS), the protocol responsible for matching websites' URLs with the numeric addresses of the servers that host them. The same content can be hosted by multiple servers with several addresses, and Kaminsky thought he had a great trick for directing users to the servers best able to handle their requests at any given moment.

Normally, DNS is reliable but not nimble. When a computer—say, a server that helps direct traffic across Comcast's network—requests the numerical address associated with a given URL, it stores the answer for a period of time known as "time to live," which can be anywhere from seconds to days. This helps to reduce the number of requests the server makes. Kaminsky's idea was to bypass the time to live, allowing the server to get a fresh answer every time it wanted to know a site's address. Consequently, traffic on Comcast's network would be sent to the optimal address at every moment, rather than to whatever address had already been stored. Kaminsky was sure that the strategy could significantly speed up content distribution.

It was only later, after talking casually about the idea with a friend, that Kaminsky realized his "trick" could completely break the security of the domain name system and, therefore, of the Internet itself. The time to live, it turns out, was at the core of DNS security; being able to bypass it allowed for a wide variety of attacks. Kaminsky wrote a little code to make sure the situation was as bad as he thought it was. "Once I saw it work, my stomach dropped," he says. "I thought, What the heck am I going to do about this? This affects everything."

Kaminsky's technique could be used to direct Web surfers to any Web page an attacker chose. The most obvious use is to send people to phishing sites (websites designed to trick people into entering banking passwords and other personal information, allowing an attacker to steal their identities) or other fake versions of Web pages. But the danger is even worse: protocols such as those used to deliver e-mail or for secure communications over the Internet ultimately rely on DNS. A creative attacker could use Kaminsky's technique to intercept sensitive e-mail, or to create forged versions of the certificates that ensure secure transactions between users and banking websites. "Every day I find another domino," Kaminsky says. "Another thing falls over if DNS is bad. . . . I mean, literally, you look around and see anything that's using a network—*anything* that's using a network—and it's probably using DNS."

Kaminsky called Paul Vixie, president of the Internet Systems Consortium, a nonprofit corporation that supports several aspects of Internet infrastructure, including the software most commonly used in the domain name system. "Usually, if somebody wants to report a problem, you expect that it's going to take a fair amount of time for them to explain it—maybe a whiteboard, maybe a Word document or two," Vixie says. "In this case, it took 20 seconds for him to explain the problem, and another 20 seconds for him to answer my objections. After that, I said, 'Dan, I am speaking to you over an unsecure cell phone. Please do not ever say to anyone what you just said to me over an unsecure cell phone again.'"

Perhaps most frightening was that because the vulnerability was not located in any particular hardware or software but in the design of the DNS protocol itself, it wasn't clear how to fix it. In secret, Kaminsky and Vixie gathered together some of the top DNS experts in the world: people from the U.S. government and high-level engineers from the major manufacturers of DNS software and hardware—companies that include Cisco and Microsoft. They arranged a meeting in March at Microsoft's campus in Redmond, WA. The arrangements were so secretive and rushed, Kaminsky says, that "there were people on jets to Microsoft who didn't even know what the bug was."

Once in Redmond, the group tried to determine the extent of the flaw and sort out a possible fix. They settled on a stopgap measure that fixed most problems, would be relatively easy to deploy, and would mask the exact nature of the flaw. Because attackers commonly identify security holes by reverse-engineering patches intended to fix them, the group decided that all its members had to release the patch simultaneously (the release date would turn out to be July 8). Kaminsky also asked security researchers not to publicly speculate on the details of the flaw for 30 days after the release of the patch, in an attempt to give companies enough time to secure their servers.

On August 6, at the Black Hat conference, the annual gathering of the world's Internet security experts, Kaminsky would publicly reveal what the flaw was and how it could be exploited.

ASKING FOR TROUBLE

Kaminsky has not really discovered a new attack. Instead, he has found an in-
genious way to breathe life into a very old one. Indeed, the basic flaw targeted by
his attack predates the Internet itself.

The foundation of DNS was laid in 1983 by Paul Mockapetris, then at the University of Southern California, in the days of ARPAnet, the U.S. Defense Department research project that linked computers at a small number of universities and
research institutions and ultimately led to the Internet. The system is designed to
work like a telephone company's 411 service: given a name, it looks up the numbers that will lead to the bearer of that name. DNS became necessary as ARPAnet
grew beyond an individual's ability to keep track of the numerical addresses in the
network.

Mockapetris, who is now chairman and chief scientist of Nomi-num, a provider of infrastructure software based in Redwood, CA, designed DNS as a hierarchy.
When someone types the URL for a Web page into a browser or clicks on a hy-
perlink, a request goes to a name server maintained by the user's Internet service
provider (ISP). The ISP's server stores the numerical addresses of URLs it handles
frequently—at least, until their time to live expires. But if it can't find an address,
it queries one of the 13 DNS root servers, which directs the request to a name
server responsible for one of the top-level domains, such as .com or .edu. That
server forwards the request to a server specific to a single domain name, such as
google.com or mit.edu. The forwarding continues through servers with ever more
specific responsibilities—mail.google.com, or libraries.mit.edu—until the request
reaches a server that can either give the numerical address requested or respond
that no such address exists.

As the Internet matured, it became clear that DNS was not secure enough. The
process of passing a request from one server to the next gives attackers many opportunities to intervene with false responses, and the system had no safeguards to
ensure that the name server answering a request was trustworthy. As early as 1989,
Mockapetris says, there were instances of "cache poisoning," in which a name
server was tricked into storing false information about the numerical address associated with a website.

In the 1990s, the poisoner's job was relatively easy. The lower-level name servers
are generally maintained by private entities: Amazon, for instance, controls the addresses supplied by the amazon.com name server. If a low-level name server can't
find a requested address, it will either refer the requester to another name server or
tell the requester the page doesn't exist. But in the 90s, the low-level server could
also furnish the requester with the top-level server's address. To poison a cache, an
attacker simply had to falsify that information. If an attacker tricked, say, an ISP's
name server into storing the wrong address for the .com server, it could hijack
most of the traffic traveling over the ISP's network.

Mockapetris says several features were subsequently added to DNS to protect the system. Requesting servers stopped accepting higher-level numerical addresses from lower-level name servers. But attackers found a way around that restriction. As before, they would refer a requester back to, say, the .com server. But now the requester had to look up the .com server's address on its own. It would request the address, and the attacker would race to respond with a forged reply before the real reply arrived. Ad hoc security measures were added to protect against this strategy, too. Now, each request to a DNS server carries a randomly generated transaction ID, one of 65,000 possible numbers, which the reply must contain as well. An attacker racing to beat a legitimate reply would also have to guess the correct transaction ID. Unfortunately, a computer can generate so many false replies so quickly that if it has enough chances, it's bound to find the correct ID. So the time to live, originally meant to keep name servers from being overburdened by too many requests, became yet another stopgap security feature. Because the requesting server will store an answer for some period of time, the attacker gets only a few chances to attempt a forgery. Most of the time, when the server needs a.com address, it consults its cache rather than checking with the .com server.

Kaminsky found a way to bypass these ad hoc security features—most important, the time to live. That made the system just as vulnerable as it was when cache poisoning was first discovered. Using Kaminsky's technique, an attacker gets a nearly infinite number of chances to supply a forgery.

Say an attacker wants to hijack all the e-mail that a social-networking site like Facebook or MySpace sends to Gmail accounts. He signs up for an account with the social network, and when he's prompted for an e-mail address, he supplies one that points to a domain he controls. He begins to log on to the social network but claims to have forgotten his password. When the system tries to send a new password, it does a DNS lookup that leads to the attacker's domain. But the attacker's server claims that the requested address is invalid.

At this point, the attacker could refer the requester to the google.com name servers and race to supply a forged response. But then he would get only one shot at cracking the transaction ID. So instead, he refers the requester to the nonexistent domains 1.google.com, then 2.google.com, then 3.google.com, and so on, sending a flood of phony responses for each. Each time, the requesting server will consult Google's name servers rather than its cache, since it won't have stored addresses for any of the phony URLs. The attack completely bypasses the limits set by the time to live. One of the attacker's forgeries is bound to get through. Then it's a simple matter to direct anything the requesting server intends for Google to the attacker's own servers, since the attacker appears to have authority for URLs ending in google.com. Kaminsky says he was able to pull off test attacks in as little as 10 seconds.

IN THE DARK

On July 8, Kaminsky held the promised press conference, announcing the release of the patch and asking other researchers not to speculate on the flaw. The hardware and software vendors had settled on a patch that forces an attacker to guess a longer transaction ID. Kaminsky says that before the patch, the attacker had to make tens of thousands of attempts to successfully poison a cache. After the patch, it would have to make billions.

News of the flaw appeared in the *New York Times*, on the BBC's website, and in nearly every technical publication. Systems administrators scrambled to get the patch worked into their systems before they could be attacked. But because Kaminsky failed to provide details of the flaw, some members of the security community were skeptical. Thomas Ptacek, a researcher at Matasano Security, posted on Twitter: "Saying it here first: doubting there's really any meat to this DNS security announcement."

Dino Dai Zovi, a security researcher best known for finding ways to deliver malware to a fully patched Macbook Pro, says, "I was definitely skeptical of the nature of the vulnerability, especially because of the amount of hype and attention versus the low amount of details. Whenever I see something like that, I instantly put on my skeptic hat, because it looks a lot like someone with a vested interest rather than someone trying to get something fixed." Dai Zovi and others noted that the timing was perfect to promote Kaminsky's Black Hat appearance, and they bristled at the request to refrain from speculation.

The lack of information was particularly controversial because system administrators are often responsible for evaluating patches and deciding whether to apply them, weighing the danger of the security flaw against the disruption that the patch will cause. Because DNS is central to the operation of any Internet-dependent organization, altering it isn't something that's done lightly. To make matters worse, this patch didn't work properly with certain types of corporate firewalls. Many IT professionals expressed frustration at the lack of detail, saying that they were unable to properly evaluate the patch when so much remained hidden.

Concerned by the skepticism about his claims, Kaminsky held a conference call with Ptacek and Dai Zovi, hoping to make them see how dangerous the bug was. Both came out of the call converted. But although Dai Zovi notes that much has changed since the time when hardware and software manufacturers dealt with flaws by simply denying that security researchers had identified real problems, he also says, "We don't know what to do when the vulnerabilities are in really big systems like DNS." Researchers face a dilemma, he says: they need to explain flaws in order to convince others of their severity, but a vulnerability like the one Kaminsky found is so serious that revealing its details might endanger the public.

Halvar Flake, a German security researcher, was one observer who thought that keeping quiet was the more harmful alternative. Public speculation is just what's needed, he says, to help people understand what could hit them. Flake read a few basic materials, including the German Wikipedia entry on DNS, and wrote a blog entry about what he thought Kaminsky might have found. Declaring that his guess was probably wrong, he invited other researchers to correct him. Somehow, amid the commotion his post caused in the security community, a detailed explanation of the flaw appeared on a site hosted by Ptacek's employer, Matasano Security. The explanation was quickly taken down, but not before it had proliferated across the Internet.

Chaos ensued. Kaminsky posted on Twitter, "DNS bug is public. You need to patch, or switch to [Web-based] Open DNS, RIGHT NOW." Within days, Metasploit, a computer security project that designs sample attacks to aid in testing, released two modules exploiting Kaminsky's flaw. Shortly after, one of the first attacks based on the DNS flaw was seen in the wild. It took over some of AT&T's servers in order to present a false Google home page, loaded with the attacker's own ads.

OUT OF COOKIES

Thirty minutes before Kaminsky took the stage at Black Hat to reveal the details of the flaw at last, people started to flood the ballroom at Caesar's Palace in Las Vegas. The speaker preceding Kaminsky hastened to wrap things up. Seats ran out, and people sat cross-legged on every square inch of carpet. Kaminsky's grandmother, who was sitting in the front row, had baked 250 cookies for the event. There were nowhere near enough.

Kaminsky walked up to the podium. "There's a lot of people out there," he said. "Holy crap." Kaminsky is tall, and his gestures are a little awkward. As of early August, he said, more than 120 million broadband customers had been protected, as Internet service providers applied patches. Seventy percent of Fortune 500 companies had patched their systems, and an additional 15 percent were working on it. However, he added, 30 to 40 percent of name servers on the Internet were still unpatched and vulnerable to his 10-second cache-poisoning attack.

Onstage, he flipped between gleeful description of his discovery's dark possibilities and attempts to muster the seriousness appropriate to their gravity. He spoke for 75 minutes, growing visibly lighter as he unburdened himself of seven months' worth of secrets. As he ended his talk, the crowd swept close to him, and he was whisked off by reporter after reporter.

Even those security experts who agreed that the vulnerability was serious were taken aback by Kaminsky's eager embrace of the media attention and his relentless effort to publicize the flaw. Later that day, Kaminsky received the Pwnie award for "most over-hyped bug" from a group of security researchers. (The word "pwn," which rhymes with "own," is Internet slang for "dominate completely." Kaminsky's award is subtitled "The Pwnie for pwning the media.") Dai Zovi, presenting the award, tried to list the publications that had carried Kaminsky's story. He gave up, saying, "What *weren't* you in?"

"*GQ!*" someone shouted from the audience.

Kaminsky took the stage and spat out two sentences: "Some people find bugs; some people get bugs fixed. I'm happy to be in the second category." Swinging the award—a golden toy pony—by its bright pink hair, he stalked down the long aisle of the ballroom and out the door.

WHO'S IN CHARGE

Depending on your perspective, the way Kaminsky handled the DNS flaw and its patch was either dangerous grandstanding that needlessly called public attention to the Internet vulnerability or—as Kaminsky sees it—a "media hack" necessary to train a spotlight on the bug's dangers. Either way, the story points to the troubling absence of any process for identifying and fixing critical flaws in the Internet. Because the Internet is so decentralized, there simply isn't a specific person or organization in charge of solving its problems.

And though Kaminsky's flaw is especially serious, experts say it's probably not the only one in the Internet's infrastructure. Many Internet protocols weren't designed for the uses they're put to today; many of its security features were tacked on and don't address underlying vulnerabilities. "Long-term, architecturally, we have to stop assuming the network is as friendly as it is," Kaminsky says. "We're just addicted to moving sensitive information across the Internet insecurely. We can do better."

Indeed, at another security conference just days after Kaminsky's presentation at Black Hat, a team of researchers gave a talk illustrating serious flaws in the Internet's routing border gateway protocol. Like Kaminsky, the researchers had found problems with the fundamental design of an Internet protocol. Like the DNS flaw, the problem could allow an attacker to get broad access to sensitive traffic sent over the Internet.

Many experts say that what happened with the DNS flaw represents the best-case scenario. Mischel Kwon, director of US-CERT, a division of the Department of Homeland Security that helped get out the word about the DNS bug, hopes the network of organizations that worked together in this case will do the same if other flaws emerge. Though there's no hierarchy of authority in the private sector, Kwon says, there are strong connections between companies and organizations with the power to deploy patches. She says she is confident that, considering the money and effort being poured into improving security on the Internet, outdated protocols will be brought up to date.

But that confidence isn't grounded in a well-considered strategy. What if Kaminsky hadn't had extensive connections within the security community or, worse, hadn't been committed to fixing the flaw in the first place? What if he had been a true "black hat" bent on exploiting the vulnerability he'd discovered? What if his seemingly skillful manipulation of the media had backfired, and the details of the flaw had become known before the patch was in place?

What's more, even given the good intentions of researchers like Kaminsky, fixing basic flaws in the Internet isn't easy. Experts agree that the DNS problem is no exception. Several proposals are on the table for solving it by means more reliable than a patch, mostly by reducing the trust a requesting server accords a name server. Proposals range from relatively simple fixes, such as including even more random information in the requests made to name servers, to moving the entire system over to a set of protocols that would let name servers sign their responses cryptographically.

In the meantime, both Kaminsky and Vixie say attackers have started to make use of the DNS flaw, and they expect more trouble to come. Kaminsky notes that the flaw becomes particularly dangerous when exploited along with other vulnerabilities. One such combination, he says, would allow an attacker to take over the automatic updates that a software vendor sends its customers, replacing them with malware. Kaminsky says he's spent the last several months on the phone to companies that would be attractive targets for that kind of attack, such as certificate authorities, social networks, and Internet service providers, trying to convince them to patch as soon as possible.

"The scary thing," Dai Zovi says, "is how fragile [the Internet] is. . . . And what are we going to do about it?"

Cybercriminals Can't Get Away With It Like They Used To[*]

Authorities Having Greater Success Tracking Them Down

By Jon Swartz
USA Today, November 17, 2008

In what is shaping up as a breakthrough year, federal authorities have quietly cracked down on some of the biggest Internet crime rings.

Secret Service and FBI operations since January have broken up a huge forum for stolen credit cards and shut down the world's largest spam ring. Investigations have led to indictments of other high-profile spammers and 11 people allegedly behind the computer break-in at TJX and other major retailers.

The FBI and Secret Service do not provide annual cybercrime statistics, but high-profile arrests are significantly up this year, says Shawn Henry, assistant director of the FBI Cyber Division.

Dozens of such actions reflect better-trained agents and prosecutors, stronger laws and more cooperation from crime fighters overseas. Strides in cybercrime fighting are particularly important now because most security experts point out that fraud soars during economic downturns. Cybercrime is an estimated $200 billion market.

For the first time, "It's not a question of whether you will be caught, but when," says Hemanshu Nigam, chief security officer of MySpace who, as a Microsoft executive, crafted a $250,000 bounty in late 2003 that led to the arrest of infamous German hacker Sven Jaschan.

Aiding the crime fighting:

- **More resources.** Federal agencies have a better understanding of technology and how to infiltrate organized crime groups, especially in Eastern Europe. "The threat is not going away. But our ability to impact the threat has become much better," says Henry.

    The Secret Service has ramped up training for its agents, prosecutors and federal judges. About 1,000 agents are trained, significantly more than a year ago. "These investigations take time and expertise," says John Large, special agent in charge of the Secret Service Criminal Investigative Division.

- **International help.** The feds are partnering closely with peers in Romania, Turkey, Germany and elsewhere. "Romania is the gold standard," says Henry, who laid the groundwork with the country's national police. Working with them, the FBI has arrested 90 people, primarily phishers, this year.

  Romanian Prosecutor General Laura Codruta Kövesi has led the effort to prosecute individuals with ties to international organized crime involved in computer and credit card fraud schemes. "The U.S. and their Romanian counterpart agencies are working as partners and colleagues," she says.

  Henry says he met with cyberofficials in Moscow in January and that Russian agents are being trained in the U.S. "We think the relationship can be as fruitful as the one in Romania," he says.

- **Stiffer cyberlaws.** Sentencing guidelines have gotten tougher. "It's easier to get someone locked up," says Keith Schwalm, president of DNK Consulting and a former Secret Service agent who worked on cybersecurity issues. One law in particular has given prosecutors a crime-fighting tool. The Identity Theft Enforcement and Restitution Act of 2008 makes it a felony to damage 10 or more PCs used by or for the federal government or a financial institution.

  Tech companies also are more aggressively pursuing criminals with existing laws. MySpace has filed five lawsuits this year against spammers, one of which resulted in a record $230 million judgment for violation of the federal anti-spam law.

Cyber-Attack Operations Near[*]

By David A. Fulghum
Aviation Week & Space Technology, January 18, 2009

In a few years, the U.S. Army, Navy and Marine Corps expect to be delivering airborne electronic fires and cyber-attacks for ground troops with a fusion of radio battalions, EA-6B Prowlers, EA-18G Growlers and a range of UAVs.

Who actually commands and controls the technology operationally and strategically remains an open question. The uncertainty was illustrated by the formation of Air Force Cyber Command, followed by its months-long pause in bureaucratic limbo and, finally, its re-designation as a numbered air force under U.S. Strategic Command. The institutional tangle was compounded because the services have still not produced a unified plan for electronic warfare and attack. It also contributed to two failures to get the Air Force back into electronic attack with an EB-52 long-range (80-100-naut.-mi.) standoff electronic attack aircraft. The design included the capability to electronically map and attack enemy networks.

"It's not about putting iron on targets anymore; it's about fighting the networks," says a U.S. EW specialist and senior technology officer. "But there is the difficulty that no one has owned cyberwarfare in the past. Now with the massive [cyber] attacks on Estonia and Georgia, it's a real threat and nobody has the charter [to combat it]."

"The organizations and lines of responsibility are still being worked," agrees Lt. Gen. Dave Deptula, the Air Force's deputy chief of staff for intelligence, surveillance and reconnaissance (ISR). "Let me be honest, we're still at the stage of understanding what cyber is. Cyber-operations broach everything from the tactical to the operational to the strategic. How it is used determines what it is.

"My opinion is that we need to normalize operations in cyber just as we've normalized operations in other domains," he says. In an air ops center, "cyberwarfare ought not to be something in a special box that is conducted somewhere else. It needs to be part of the equation in determining a regional contingency plan in equal fashion just like air, space, maritime and ground components."

As cyber- and electronic attack technologies emerge, it is becoming harder to distinguish between cyberwarfare, directed energy and electronic attack, intelligence gathering and information operations. Rationalization of all these elements also is complicated by shrinking manpower and funding.

Meanwhile, there is the new concept of "hybrid warfare," a term coined by U.S. Joint Forces Command. Characteristics of hybrid war are a "very dynamic, uncertain environment [that creates] a lot of change and persistent conflict," says Vice Adm. Robert Harward, the deputy commander of USJFC. The command's operational predictions include increasing dependence on unmanned sensors and aircraft and small fighting units that will employ directed-energy and cyber-weapons.

What the military will look like in 10–15 years "is a little bit of a mystery and may be a little bit of a secret," Defense Secretary Robert Gates told troops in Southwest Asia. But the conflicts in that region are producing templates for future combat—in particular, "the marriage of combat operations and ISR, the ability to dwell over a target, and the ability for relatively small units to have situational awareness of what's going on [around them]," he says. "I think this use of ISR and the integration of intelligence and operations is something we will see continue. This is revolutionizing the way we fight."

Gates bemoans the fact that in some areas first-world nations are already falling behind the insurgents. "How did we end up in a place where the country that invented public relations is being out-communicated by a guy in a cave? Partly, we are still operating too much in a 20th century mind-set."

Air Force officials managing the intersection of ISR, cyberwar, directed energy and information operations echo that concern.

"We need new capabilities to deal with [the enemy's use of advanced technology]," says Deptula. But making the job more difficult is "more demand and fewer resources," he adds. "So we've got to come up with some new approaches. What makes the most sense, given that we're [also] reducing in size?" Part of the answer is high-speed technologies—such as cyberwarfare and high-power microwave (HPM) weapons, he says. But learning to employ them and assign responsibility for their use is still a work in progress.

"As we move from speed-of-sound to speed-of-light weapons, we're beginning to see the changes required to deal with cyber-operations," says Deptula. "HPM is going to be another game-changing capability. We're not there yet, but . . . those capabilities are coming out of ISR, so we have to move rapidly to adapt our organizations to integrate those kinds of weapons. What's critical is to create the command relationships and authority to capitalize on those weapons and not restrict their capabilities.

"Every service ought to have some sort of cyber-component that organizes, trains and equips to how they present force capabilities for combatant commanders," he says. "Then we have a common definition that each of the services can shape to operationally fit their basic core competencies for conduct of military operations in a regional scenario."

As these capabilities are introduced, joint operations are expected to undergo fundamental changes.

"We see a [future] environment that is very much focused on distributed, decentralized, leader-centric and network-enabled [units and] structures [placed] throughout the joint forces," says Harward, who is a Navy Seal and former director of special reconnaissance and direct-action missions in Afghanistan and Iraq. Those special ops-like units will be trained to "have the ability to operate with the commander's intent when systems fail and they can't get information," he says.

Joint Forces Command also embraces the quick introduction of advanced weaponry.

"Everybody recognizes that electronic fires [such as jamming, directed energy and cyberwar] is a capability that ought to be bought, maintained and developed," says Harward. "It's part of the technology advantage that we have right now, and our ability to expand it will pay dividends. We're looking at it in the experimentation phase and how we might move forward."

Training for the hybrid war also is likely to look different. Planners want high-fidelity, fighter aircraft-like simulators for ground soldiers so that responses to attacks, ambushes and other encounters are well rehearsed before anyone is thrust into combat. Simulators would also allow operational lessons learned to be immediately fed back into the training.

However, researchers are worried that pieces of the digital puzzle are still missing—in particular, projection of new threats that foes may throw at the U.S.

"As you go into a new theater of operations, you see [advanced communications and new uses for networks] pop-up everywhere," he says. "The threat is there, ad hoc, undefined and asymmetric. So you have to stand up your capability quickly to defend and fight your networks. It's changing the way we think about deploying software-defined radios [for example]. We're using common modules that have software functions that are adaptable in real time as the threat changes."

There also are no digital weapons that can be used by nonspecialists, and there is no ability to duplicate networks so attacks and exploitation can be planned and practiced. As a result, the Defense Advanced Research Projects Agency awarded seven six-month contracts totaling about $25 million as startup funding for a National Cyber Range (NCR). The move is being applauded by military officials, who shared their insights into the effort.

It would be the nation's premier cyber-test facility. Candidates would have to provide a complete, integrated system, and Darpa will not act as the integrator.

Test analyses are to be unbiased and quantitative assessments of information assurance and survivability tools. The laboratory is to replicate complex, large-scale networks for current and future Defense Dept. weapons and operations.

The capabilities to be tested are host security systems, local-area network security tools and suites, wide-area network systems operating on unusual bandwidths, tactical networks (including the problematic mobile ad hoc networks) and new protocol stacks.

To further hedge their bets, Darpa officials may fund multiple teams to simultaneously build competing prototype NCRs. Testing of the ranges will include demonstration of "packet capture" and automated attacks. Flexibility and adaptation will likely be the key concept to winning the technology wars, just as it is in conventional combat.

"We don't know if knocking down more walls in the intelligence [world], conducting cyber-operations and introducing nonkinetic weapons like HPM are going to be sequential problems, or if they will all arrive together," says Deptula.

"I'd like us to accelerate our ability to meet some of the challenges we have with directed-energy weapons because they certainly will be game-changing," he adds. "Once a capability is fielded and begins to be employed, there's a lot to learn between what was anticipated and what actually takes place. Our organizations must evolve accordingly."

Bibliography

Books

Abram, Carolyn and Pearlman, Leah. *Facebook for Dummies*. Indianapolis: Wiley Publishing, Inc., 2008

Bast, Donna. *Teens and Computers . . . What's a Parent to Do?: A Basic Guide to Social Networking, Instant Messaging, Chat, Email, Computer Set-up and More*. Charleston: BookSurge Publishing, 2007

Chap, Clark, et. al. *Disconnected: Parenting Teens in a MySpace World*. Cambridge: Baker Books, 2007

Criddle, Linda. *Look Both Ways: Help Protect Your Family on the Internet*. Seattle: Microsoft Press, 2006

Croner, Douglas E. *The Internet Book: Everything You Need to Know About Computer Networking and How the Internet Works*. Upper Saddle Road: Prentice Hall, 2007

Crovella, Mark and Krishnamurthy, Balachander. *Internet Measurement: Infrastructure, Traffic and Applications*. Indianapolis: Wiley Publishing, Inc., 2006

Gantz, John and Rochester, Jack B. *Pirates of the Digital Millennium: How the Intellectual Property Wars Damage Our Personal Freedoms, Our Jobs, and the World Economy*. FT Press, 2004

Goldsmith, Jack and Wu, Tim. *Who Controls the Internet?: Illusions of a Borderless World*. New York: Oxford University Press, 2008

Goodman, Danny. *Spam Wars: Our Last Best Chance to Defeat Spammers, Scammers & Hackers*. New York: Select Books, 2004

Goodstein, Anastasia. *Totally Wired: What Teens and Tweens Are Really Doing Online*. New York: St. Martin's Griffin Press, 2007

Gralla, Preston and Lindley, Eric. *How Personal & Internet Security Work*. London: Que, 2006

Hallam-Baker, Phillip. *DotCrime Manifesto: How to Stop Internet Crime*. Boston: Pearson Technology Group, 2008

Haugen, Hayley Mitchell and Musser, Susan. *Internet Safety (Issues That Concern You)*. Farmington Hills: Greenhaven Press, 2008

Hinduja, Sameer and Patchin, Justin W.. *Bullying Beyond the Schoolyard: Preventing and Respond-

ing to Cyberbullying. Thousand Oaks: Corwin Press, 2008

Hupfer, Ryan. *MySpace for Dummies.* Indianapolis: Wiley Publishing, Inc., 2008

Jones, David Kent. *Online Teen Dangers: The Five Greatest Internet Dangers Teenagers Face and What You Can Do to Protect Them.* CreateSpace, 2008

Jordan, Tim. *Hacktivism and Cyberwars: Rebels with a Cause.* London: Routledge, 2004

Kelly, Richard V. *Massively Multiplayer Online Role-Playing Games: The People, the Addiction and the Playing Experience.* Jefferson: McFarland & Company, 2004

Kelsey, Candice M. *Generation MySpace: Helping Your Teen Survive Online Adolescence.* Washington, D.C.: Marlowe & Company, 2007

Kern, Jan. *Eyes Online, Eyes On Life: A Journey Out of Online Obsession.* Cincinnati: Standard Publishing Company, 2008

Leavitt, Jacalyn and Linford, Sally. *Faux Paw's Adventures in the Internet: Keeping Children Safe Online.* Indianapolis: Wiley Publishing, Inc., 2006

Magid, Larry and Collier, Anne. *MySpace Unraveled: A Parent's Guide to Teen Social Networking.* Berkeley: Peachpit Press, 2008

Magid, Larry and Collier, Anne. *MySpace Unraveled: A Parent's Guide to Teen Social Networking.* Berkeley: Peachpit Press, 2006

McWilliams, Brian S. *Spam Kings: The Real Story behind the High-Rolling Hucksters Pushing Porn, Pills, and %*@)# Enlargements.* Sebastopol: O'Reilly Media, Inc., 2004

Mehan, Julie E. *Cyberwar, Cyberterror, CyberCrime.* Cambridgeshire: IT Governance, Ltd. 2008

Nagy, Dennis. *Dating 911: Internet Dating Safety.* Bloomington: AuthorHouse, 2003

Osit, Michael. *Generation Text: Raising Well-Adjusted Kids in an Age of Instant Everything.* New York: AMACOM, 2008

Our Personal Freedoms, Our Jobs, and the World Economy. Upper Saddle River: Prentice Hall, 2005

Peltier, Thomas R., et. al. *Information Security Fundamentals.* Boca Raton: Auerbach Publications, 2005

Reid, Paul. *Biometrics for Network Security.* Upper Saddle River: Prentice Hall, 2004

Slade, Robert M.. *Software Forensics.* New York: McGraw-Hill, 2004

Vacca, John R. *Practical Internet Security.* New York: Springer, 2006

Verton, Dan. *The Hacker Diaries: Confessions of Teenage Hackers.* New York: McGraw-Hill Professional, 2002

Walker, Andy. *Absolute Beginner's Guide to Security, Spam, Spyware, & Viruses.* London: Que, 2005

Willard, Nancy E. and Steiner, Karen. *Cyberbullying and Cyberthreats: Responding to the Challenge of Online Social Aggression, Threats, and Distress.* Champaign: Research Press, 2007

Web sites

The following Web sites contain additional information about Internet safety, all of which were operational as of this writing.

CyberAngels

www.cyberangels.org

CyberAngels is an Internet safety program developed by the Guardian Angels, the international volunteer organization of unarmed crime fighters. Founded in 1995, it is one of the oldest online safety education programs. It is a comprehensive site featuring many articles and resources about online safety, especially for children and teenagers.

Federal Trade Commission: Fighting Back Against Identity Theft

www.ftc.gov/bcp/edu/microsites/idtheft/index.html

Created by the President's Task Force on Identity Theft in 2006, this Web site was designed to educate the public about identity theft. It contains articles, videos, and a host of information for detecting and deterring identity theft. One can also use the site to report identity theft to the FTC.

U.S. Office of Personel Management: Federal Cyber Service

www.sfs.opm.gov

The U.S. Office of Personnel Management, funded by the National Science Foundation, is giving scholarships to students interested in a career in internet security. This program is designed to train professionals to protect the government's information infrastructure. Included are information and applications for participants.

National Institute of Standards and Technology

www.nist.gov

The NIST is a federal agency that promotes U.S. innovation and industrial competitiveness through advancing measurement science, standards, and technology. It is a branch of the U.S. Department of Commerce and its headquarters are in Maryland with a laboratory in Colorado. The NIST is also home to the Comprehensive National Cybersecurity Initiative, which is a government to secure government networks.

WiredKids, Inc. and WiredSafety.org

www.wiredkids.com

www.wiredsafety.org

Created by cyberspace lawyer Parry Aftab, WiredKids, Inc. and WiredSafety.org provide extensive information about cybercrimes—such as cyberbullying, child pornography, and identity theft—specifically directed to children and teenagers.

NetSmartz Workshop

www.netsmartz.org

NetSmartz Workshop is an online educational resource created jointly by the National

Center for Missing & Exploited Children (NCMEC) and Boys & Girls Clubs of America (BGCA). Using interactive features and extensive articles, NetSmartz Workshop carries a breadth of information on internet safety for children, parents, educators, and law enforcement agents.

Megan Meier Foundation

www.meganmeierfoundation.org

A non-profit organization to educate children, parents, and educators in order to counter bullying—cyber and otherwise. It is dedicated to Megan Meier, the 13-year-old girl who committed suicide after being cyberbullied. Included are online resources, media clips, volunteer opportunities, a bio of Tina Meier (Megan's mother), a link to give donations to the foundation, contacts, and a link for inviting Mrs. Meier to a speaking engagement.

Teenangels.org

www.teenangels.org

Teenangels are teenage volunteers who are trained in on-line safety. They inform their peers in programs in schools across the nation. Included on the site are Internet safety tips, a form to create a Teenangel chapter, a form to volunteer, and other on-line safety information.

Internet Security Presentations

www.securitypresentations.com

A blog, Internet Security Presentations contains online security information in individual slideshow presentations. Topics include securing systems, Web connection security, identity theft, and many more.

i-Safe, Inc.

www.isafe.org

i-Safe is a nonprofit foundation created to educate youth and parents about online safety. Included on the Web site are links to educational resources and news, as well as information for children, parents, law enforcement, and educators. The Web site also features five online educational program modules for students, parents, mentors, law enforcers, and

adults called iLearn.

Additional Periodical Articles with Abstracts

More information about Internet safety and related subjects can be found in the following articles. Readers interested in additional articles may consult the *Readers' Guide to Periodical Literature* and other H.W. Wilson publications.

E-Buyer Beware: Why Online Auction Fraud Should Be Regulated. Miriam R. Albert. *American Business Law Journal*, pp575-643, Summer 2002.

In this article, part of a special issue on cyberlaw, Albert discusses how the increasing use of the Internet as a medium of commerce has led to an increase in Internet fraud, raising new and challenging legal issues in areas including online auctions. Under current law, a defrauded participant in an online auction transaction has no recourse against the online auction site. However, the author contends, the FTC should apply its substantial regulatory authority to the creation of binding regulations for online auction sites. Such regulations should include ideas such as authenticating participants' identities, limiting the number of user names per participant, verifying the creditworthiness of participants, offering insurance for the full amount of transactions, offering authentication of items for sale, and establishing mandatory record-keeping provisions, together with all other measures necessary to provide the highest level of consumer protection possible.

Simple Security. James Fallows. *Atlantic Monthly*, pp144+, October 2007.

Safeguarding a computer against viruses and similar problems is like defending a country against bombings and similar terrorist threats, Fallows observes. Worrying too little about the threat leaves one exposed to risk, while worrying too much can lead to the sacrifice of the very things one sought to protect, such as flexibility, freedom, and simple peace of mind. In personal computing, however, users have the tools to protect themselves without endangering other necessities. Fallows presents an overview of some of these tools, along with guidelines about which threats are grave enough to worry about.

Get a Virtual Life. *Current Health 2*, pp26–29, November 2008.

Online interactive worlds provide teenagers with the opportunity to share their experiences with other teenagers around the globe and offer endless potential for adventure, exploration, and social interaction, the writer notes, but there are risks associated with such opportunities. Kimberly Young, director of the Center for Internet Addiction Recovery and a professor at St. Bonaventure University in New York, notes that social relationships are sometimes hindered in real life because teenagers are so busy cultivating relationships online. Although interacting with new friends from around the world can be exciting, online buddies should not replace real-life friends. Furthermore, if teenagers ever feel that their involvement with virtual worlds may be developing into an addiction, they should ask a friend, family member, or counselor for help.

Your Child and the Internet: Tips to Keep Them Safe on the Information Superhighway. Monica Jones. *Ebony*, pp130+, March 2006.

Although the Internet can be a valuable educational tool with limitless benefits, children who use it are at risk of encountering such dangers as sexual predators, pornography, and sites promoting racial hatred, Jones observes. Everyone can publish or access information on the Web, and preteens and teens are at the greatest risk because of the increased likelihood that their online activities will be unsupervised. Advice is provided for parents on protecting their children when using the Internet.

Cyberbullying by Adolescents: A Preliminary Assessment. Paris S. and Robert D. Strom, *The Educational Forum*, pp21–36, Fall 2005.

A new threat has arisen for which teachers, administrators, and parents admit they are poorly prepared. Cyberbullying—electronic forms of peer harassment—is becoming increasingly prevalent and often originates beyond the legal reach of the school. This presentation describes how cyberbullying differs from other forms of mistreatment, cites examples of Internet intimidation, identifies procedures for responding to electronic threats, explores implications for teachers and parents, recommends questions for initial research, and presents a poll for schools to use in assessing student experience with cyberbullying.

Fear of a Black Hat. Adam L. Penenberg. *Fast Company*, pp51–52+, July/August 2008.

"Black Hat" hacking is when hackers sell "odays" or recipes and a code for penetrating the software run by governments, corporations, and private citizens, Penenberg explains. When properly deployed, odays can lead to minor disruptions such as the temporary paralysis of a Web site. Penenberg likewise discusses the black market trade in hacker code.

Child Pornography Web Sites: Techniques Used to Evade Law Enforcement. Wade Luders. *FBI Law Enforcement Bulletin*, pp17–21, July 2007.

The writer outlines the techniques that those operating child pornography Web sites use to evade law enforcement's efforts to capture them. These include using proxy servers, hiding the location of the illegal content, using uniform resource locator (URL) encoding techniques, pretending to be located in another country, using Internet protocol (IP) filters, and providing anonymous payment methods. Awareness of such methods is vital for law enforcement agencies in their struggle to combat a critical international problem.

Parental Influence and Teens' Attitude Toward Online Privacy Protection. Seounmi Youn. *The Journal of Consumer Affairs*, pp362–88, Fall 2008.

In this study, Youn examines the impact of parental influence on teens' attitude toward privacy protection. Survey data show that teens high in concept-oriented family communication tend to engage in discussion mediation, which, in turn, affects their level of privacy concern. In contrast, teens high in socio-oriented communication tend to have more family rules and surf the Internet with parents. Rulemaking mediation is not directly related to teens' level of privacy concern, while cosurfing mediation is related to their level of concern. This study also finds that parental mediation and teens' concern level explain their attitude toward privacy protection measures. Implications for policymakers and educators are discussed.

The Secret Network of Child Predators. Brian Bethune. *Maclean's*, pp32–36+, April 23, 2007.

Just as it has proved for millions of ordinary individuals, the Internet has become the greatest empowering tool pedophiles have ever had, Bethune contends. According to investigative journalist Julian Sher, this means that a proclivity that has always been part of the human condition is now getting much worse in terms of both magnitude and severity. Sher says that although it does not create pedophilia, the Internet certainly does fuel it. Worst of all, in Sher's opinion, the Web drags in men and women who probably would not have otherwise. For proof of this, one only has to think of the case of Michael Briere, who raped and murdered ten-year-old Holly Jones. An excerpt from Sher's book *One Child At a Time: The Global Fight to Rescue Children from Online Predators* is presented.

You've Got Spam. Derek Chezzi. *Maclean's*, pp30–34, February 23, 2004.

Regardless of how many times one changes e-mail addresses or switches Internet service providers, Chezzi reports, it is impossible to escape the unsolicited messages known as spam. Over the past ten years, e-mail has developed into an invaluable form of international communication, but the amount of unwanted messages has skyrocketed, with antispam technology firm Brightmail Inc. estimating that spam accounts for 60 percent of all e-mails sent, four times more than it did two years ago. Recently, the Organization for Economic Co-operation and Development held a meeting in Brussels to consider the fight against spam. There, the EU argued that because the United States is the biggest source of unwanted commercial bulk e-mail, it should be doing more to combat the problem.

Thieves Winning Online War, Maybe Even in Your Computer. John Markoff. *New York Times*, ppA1, A14, December 6, 2008.

The onslaught of malware worldwide is spreading faster than ever and computer security experts admit that they are losing the battle, Markoff reports. An estimated $100 billion a year is lost to a thriving criminal economy practicing credit card thefts, bank fraud and other scams. With their illegal profits, criminal gangs are rapidly improving their technology. They are headquartered in countries that have little interest in prosecuting crimes that bring significant amounts of foreign currency into the country. As the criminal element thrives, many Internet executives fear that the public's trust in the Internet as a foundation of commercial activity is eroding.

Sending E-Mail in a Spam-Hysterical World. David A. Karp. *PC Magazine*, pp103–04, October 2008.

The torrent of spam can spell trouble for outgoing mail, Karp observes. What was once a manageable stream of pornographic invitations, baldness remedies, and laughable stock tips has developed into a flood of nonsensical detritus laced with spyware and malware. When an ISP fights back, it can mean problems for outgoing messages. For example, early this year, AT&T impetuously began to block all e-mail from any IP address identified as a source of even one spam message. Thousands of legitimate e-mails were returned to their senders or simply dumped, and the intended recipients never knew about it. Karp also provides tips on keeping up with ISPs' efforts to block spam while ensuring that messages get through.

Thwarting Identity Theft. Matthew D. Sarrel. *PC Magazine*, p96, November 2008.

The number of cases of identity theft is decreasing, but people still need to protect themselves, Sarrel reports. The number of identity theft victims per annum in the United States fell from 10.1 million to 8.4 million from 2003 to 2007, according to a Javelin Strategy & Research survey, as reported by the Privacy Rights Clearinghouse. Furthermore, the average time required to undo the damage in each case was down from 40 hours in 2006 to 25 in 2007. Even these falling numbers are fairly high, however, and learning that one's credit card has been used by a stranger can be chilling. Sarrel also offers advice on how to protect against identity theft.

Don't Be Dragooned Into the Botnet Army. Erik Larkin. *PC World*, pp47–48, December 2008.

According to Larkin, there has been a steep increase in the number of computers corralled into botnets—far-flung networks of infected PCs that digital crooks use to steal financial account data, relay spam, and launch crippling Internet attacks. Now that popular Web sites can invisibly and unwillingly spread malicious software, the days of staying safe just by being careful as to where one surfs are unfortunately long gone. Nonetheless, Larkin discusses the steps Web users can take to protect themselves and their PCs from these threats.

Hand-to-Keyboard Combat. Henry Schlesinger. *Popular Science*, pp33–34, November 2008.

The U.S. government has set up a new Internet security division to deal with cybercrime, Schlesinger reports. Attacks against government computers are escalating at an alarming rate worldwide. In an effort to coordinate countermeasures against such cyberterrorism, the Department of Homeland Security has launched the National Cyber Security Center (NCSC), part of the semiclassified, $17-billion Comprehensive National Cybersecurity Initiative (CNCI) formed by presidential directive in January. The NCSC's mission is to monitor, analyze, and distribute data related to attacks on government networks, and the organization will be headed up by former Silicon Valley entrepreneur Rod Beckstrom. While Beckstrom and his team are fighting cyberterrorism, other arms of the CNCI will look at potential security threats within the federal computer system.

Cyberbullying: Is There Anything Schools Can Do? Kelley R. Taylor. *Principal Leadership*, pp60–62, May 2008.

The writer discusses what schools can do about cyberbullying. School officials can discipline students for cyberbullying that occurs on campus; however, the Web sites and e-mails that are involved in cyberbullying are usually accessed and generated by students off-campus, which means school officials are limited in what, if anything, they can do to punish such behavior. The myriad cases dealing with school officials' attempts to discipline students for inappropriate off-campus speech in recent years are all different, which highlights how difficult it is to delineate school officials' authority to restrict, regulate, or otherwise discipline students' speech that occurs off school grounds. However, well-developed school policy and school officials' proper action in accordance with those policies can make a difference; therefore, many states have embraced legislation that requires schools to add cyberbullying to their anti-harassment policies.

E-commerce Regulation: New Game, New Rules? Carlos A. Primo Braga. *Quarterly Review of Economics and Finance*, pp541-58, 2005.

Policymakers face many challenges in laying the foundations of a sound regulatory environment for e-commerce, Braga observes. These challenges reflect not only the large variety of policies that can influence e-commerce, but also the emergence of new governance issues that require international coordination. Moreover, the rapid expansion of networks has increased the potential for cross-border disputes in this area. Braga argues that competition among national regulatory regimes is unlikely to promote regulatory harmonization in the near future. The negotiation of a new set of rules at the multilateral level, however, is bound to proceed at a slower pace than what would be desirable from the perspective of e-commerce firms. The paper points out that the WTO—as an obvious organization to advance the agenda of multilateral disciplines—is not in a position to deliver quick results with respect to e-commerce. The main contribution that the WTO can offer at this stage concerns the expansion of commitments under the GATS, fostering national treatment and broader market access, particularly in telecommunications and computer-related services.

Chinese Computer Hackers. Simon Elegant. *Time*, pp56–58, December 17, 2007.

Some people believe that the Chinese government may be creating an army of Internet warriors, Elegant reports. Chinese computer hackers are allegedly breaking into high-security networks in America and other nations. China has long viewed cyberwarfare as a vital component of asymmetrical warfare in any future conflict with America. From China's perspective, it makes sense to employ any means possible to counter America's massive technological advantage. The current wave of hacking attacks appears to be aimed largely at collecting information and probing defenses. In a real cyberwar, however, a successful attack would be aimed at computer-dependent infrastructure, including banking and power generation.

Next Steps in Defense Restructuring. Jacques S. Gansler. *Issues in Science and Technology*, 67–70, Summer 2003.

The U.S. military needs to shift its focus to nontraditional areas, Gansler contends. During the 1980s, the security forces were organized to face a land attack in Europe from a Warsaw Pact country or a nuclear submarine attack on U.S. cities. The security environment has changed from a cold war to a war against terror, with future adversaries likely to use asymmetrical approaches, such as suicide bombers, that are not deterred or contained by conventional U.S. military might. The military thus needs to shift its resources, training, organizations, and equipment into nontraditional areas that include special operations forces, urban warfare, and defense against battlefield use of weapons of mass destruction, ballistic missiles, and cyberwarfare. Bringing about the needed changes will be neither rapid nor easy, but sufficient resources to pay for such changes can be generated out of current defense budgets.

Thief vs. Patient. Michelle Andrews. *U.S. News & World Report*, pp48-49, March 17, 2008.

At a time when the push toward electronic medical records is gaining momentum, privacy experts are concerned that there may be a substantial increase in the occurrence of medical identity theft, Andrews reports. For victims of such theft, the result can be thousands in unpaid charges, damaged credit, and false, possibly dangerous, details cluttering up their medical records for years to come. In some cases of medical identity theft, employees inside the health care system are stealing patients' information in order to make bogus insurance claims. It can be difficult to untangle the mess created by theft of this nature because there is no straightforward process for challenging false medical claims or correcting inaccurate medical records. The best first line of defense against medical identity theft may be the patients themselves.

Make It Predator-Proof. Michelle Andrews. *U.S. News & World Report*, p52, September 18, 2006.

In this piece, part of a special section on MySpace.com, the writer offers advice for parents on ensuring that a child uses MySpace.com safely: Ask the child to go through his or her account details, remove identifying details or photographs, ensure the child's photo is not overly sexual or suggestive, eliminate text that indicates the child is emotionally vulnerable, use protection features offered by MySpace, read friends' profiles to ensure they are not putting the child at risk, and talk to children about what they are doing to help them develop their critical thinking.

When Play Turns to Trouble. Jennifer Seter Wagner. *U.S. News & World Report*, pp51-53, May 19, 2008.

Concern is spreading among parents and mental-health professionals that the ever-increasing popularity of computer and video games has a darker side. Wagner observes. The Media Research Lab at Iowa State University reports that around 8.5 percent of 8-to-18-year-old gamers can be considered pathologically addicted, and almost one-quarter of young people concede they have felt addicted. Kimberly Young, director of the Center for Internet Addiction Recovery, notes several common warning signs of pathological behavior: fantasizing or talking about game characters or missions when offline, lying about or hiding how much time is spent playing, disobeying parental restrictions, losing interest in sports and hobbies, choosing the game over time with friends, and playing despite slumping grades, loss of a scholarship, or a breakup with a partner. Finding effective professional help for this addiction can be difficult, however, because game addiction is not currently recognized by the American Psychiatric Association.

Index